PETRA

AN ARCHAEOLOGICAL GUIDE.
HISTORY, CIVILISATION AND MONUMENTS

FABIO BOURBON

MAGNUS

Distributed in Jordan by: **Redwan book shop**
Tel: +962 3 2013704, Fax: +962 3 2015588
email: redwanbook@hotmail.com
Printed 2014

PETRA

AN ARCHAEOLOGICAL GUIDE. HISTORY, CIVILISATION AND MONUMENTS

Project, texts, pagination
FABIO BOURBON

Photographs
FABIO BOURBON AND ANGELA WHITE

Drawings
MONICA FALCONE BOURBON

CONTENTS

Editorial coordination:
Whitelight, Vercelli, Italy, www.whitelight.com
Photolito:
Digipress – Romano Canavese (Province of Turin)
Printing:
Lito Terrazzi Srl – Cascine del Riccio (Province of Florence)
Translation: www.accademiadellelingue.it

2007 ©MAGNUS EDIZIONI SpA, UDINE, ITALY

ISBN 88-7057-209-9 English edition

I wish to especially thank Suleyman Farjat, the director of Petra's
archaeological area, for his priceless availability, and Sami
Mohammed Al Nawafleh, the archaeologist who illustrated the
most recent discoveries to me . My heartfelt thanks also go to all
those – Petra's current dwellers – who in various ways helped me
during my long days of exploration (and to whom I hereby express
my excuses should I have inaccurately or wrongly transliterated
their names): Bedoul Mofleh, Ahmed al Bedoul, Yuned Kaled al
Bedoul, Mohammed Ahudè Eyud, Ibrahim Mohammed al Bedoul,
Yunis Kaled Salamè. My thanks also to Angela White, an excellent
photographer and matchless companion of adventures. To end
with, all my gratitude goes to my wife Monica, without whom all
this would not have been possible.

F.B.

INTRODUCTION

A lot of writers throughout history tried to shed light on the majestic ancient city of Petra and the mighty builders that diligently crafted its breathtaking façades. Each tool used to carve each inch of this city had a story to tell.

We know from historians and scholars that this city was built by the Nabataean Arabs that used to dwell in this area since the dawn of time. Some say they are descendants of the Edomites, some say they came from North Arabia, but truly until this minute we do not have enough evidence to pin point their origins or even where they ended up at, but what we know for sure is that they have left prints of their existence on every rock they touched.

The visitor to this ancient city will be able to experience the power of civilizations that past. As one wanders through its narrow gorges and vast areas you can clearly see how the Nabataeans were influenced by Mesopotamia, Persia, Egypt, Greece and later Rome.

This book is merely a tool to help you explore the beauty of this truly fascinating experience where you will be able to touch on a civilization that left its echoes through history. Welcome to the land of the Nabataeans, welcome to the land of our ancestors.

His Excellency Engineer Nader Dahabi,
Chief Commissioner, Aqaba Special Economic
Zone Authority

1 Petra's first name was Reqem, namely the multicoloured [city].

2-3 The spectacular mole of el Deir, or Monastery,

4-5 Overall view of the "Royal Tombs".

7 The Tomb of the Obelisks and the underlying Bab el Siq Triclinium.

8-9 The symbol itself of Petra, i.e., the superb and extremely smart façade of el Khazneh, seen from the Siq' s gloomy ravine.

PREFACE

I fell in love with Petra when I first saw it, and now, after so many years, every time I have the honour to revisit it, I still feel like a young boy at his first date. Though I have toured the world, I haven't been everywhere, yet, without hesitation I believe I can say that it is absolutely unique. Petra is one of those rare places where, even people who do not believe in magic, quite soon must revise their convictions. If you are able to grasp its charm – by listening to the poetry of silence, by gazing at the kaleidoscopic, ceaseless change in colours, while admiring the superb balance of the rock-cut architecture – even you shall be paid back by the intimate, profound feeling of a matchless beauty. Above all, you shall go back home storing a treasure in your hearts.

The ancient Nabataean capital, with its multi-coloured rocks and the extraordinary structures - carved, sculptured and engraved in sandstone two thousands years ago-, extends on an very vast area. Thus, it would be presumptuous to state that this guide illustrates each of its monuments, every corner. For certain, it was written with sincere dedication, and I hope it shall be useful to you while you approach the Red-rose City and its marvels.

In these pages, I privileged the practical aspect, leaving the deepening of the historical events, of the art and culture underlying Nabataean civilisation and Petra itself to much more adequate texts (or to the reading of my previous guide, which, though not very recent, I believe is still valid). Far from being exhaustive, in all cases I think this booklet may serve visitors as a useful tool for starting the exploration of the archaeological area with their own means and a solid foundation. Texts are short, all information is updated to the best of my knowledge, all itineraries I verified personally and the images are, per se, more explanatory than any word.

As they say around here, *ahlan wa sahlan*: welcome!

F. B.

A LITTLE HISTORY

Above all, as was said before, this is a handy guide for a visit to the Pink City. A short historical introduction, however, is always necessary; all the same, data concerning the Nabataean civilisation shall be privileged. For further deepening, please refer to the authoritative texts quoted in the bibliography.

Set in southern Jordan, about 300 km south of Amman, Petra is quoted in the Bible as Sela' – the Jewish equivalent of "Rock", whilst Petra is its Greek translation. Not all historians, however, agree in giving the rocky city such place name, since another locality so called rises about 40 km north of Petra. Little information can be garnered in other two historical sources, the *Bibliotheca* by Diodorus Siculus (ca. 90-20 b.C.), and the *Geographia*, by Strabo (64 b.C.-23 A.D. approx.), both describing the city as the sumptuous capital of the Nabataeans, nomadic folk who got rich thanks to caravan trade;

Diodorus remarks that said people got to this land shortly after the demise of Alexander the Great (occurring in 323 b.C.). Today we know that before their arrival, during the Palaeolithic, the whole area had already been inhabited by groups of hunters and pickers, who roamed unceasingly in their quest for food. In a zone known as al Beidha, a few km from Petra, the remains of a human settlement, dated as 9000 b.C., were discovered; in both the Chalcolithic and the Bronze Age (4000-2500 b.C.) camps of nomads and villages of farmers, by then permanent, coexisted in the territory. In the two following millenniums the region was probably struck by climatic upsets, and many villages were forthwith abandoned, so much so that just a few, sporadic groups of nomads kept on wandering in the environs. Only during the Iron Age a human group returned to settle permanently in Petra's hollow, castling on the very top of a rocky

10 Left: from the summit of Umm al Biyara- the stronghold dominating Petra's entire hollow-, our gaze ventures west, until it reaches the huge wadi Arabah depression, where the Nabataean copper mines are located.

10 Centre: the map shows the main caravan routes that led to Petra.

10 Right: rocky inscription near Gebel Attuf: the language that the Nabataeans spoke belonged to the Semitic stock.

11 Left: remains of an Edomite settlement on the top of Umm al Biyara.

11 Right: this image recalls the time when large caravans reached the Nabataean capital.

emergence known as al Habis. Around the XII century, the Edomites, a people of Semitic stock, managed to take over the lands lying between the Dead Sea and the Gulf of Aqaba; for a long time, relations between the latter and the neighbouring Israelites were difficult, if not the worst possible. Especially after the fall of Jerusalem at the hand of the Babylonians (587 b.C.), the Edomites repeatedly attacked and looted the kingdom of Judah; however,

the latter were already enduring the pressure exerted by a nomadic and determined people, coming from the Arabic peninsula: the Nabataeans. These, in turn, were driven more and more north-west by Babylonian expansion. Though their exact place of origin be still unknown, they were surely resolute and laborious folks, who managed quite quickly to give up the restricted ambits of a nomadic society and successfully enter a much wider system of political and economic relations: already at the end of the IV century b.C., caravans of Nabataean merchants went from Arabia as far as the Mediterranean along a north-south axis, and from Syria to Egypt treading on the west-bound routes from the east. In their commercial activities they used Aramaic, the merchant language then spoken throughout the Near East. Described in the earliest reliable historical documents as desert dwellers, devoted to sheep-breeding and unaware of agriculture, unable to build housing and wine-despisers, they forthwith and drastically changed their own way of life, even if the various stages of this epochal transformation remain unfathomed. For certain, the land occupied by the Nabataeans provided scanty resources, i.e., only a few copper mines along the Wadi Arabah (the huge depression of the Earth's surface connecting the Dead Sea and the Gulf of Aqaba, on whose southern versant lies

the valley of Petra) and the bitumen of the Dead Sea, which was exported into Egypt as a raw material for mummifying the dead. The Nabataean caravans were immense, so much so to appear to historian Strabo as real armies on the move; Nabataean commercial ability lay in their ability in detecting what the most precious and sought after goods were in the countries set along the routes of communication. In southern Arabia, in today's Yemen, they bought myrrh, incense and spices that they eventually sold at dear prices at Gaza, Alexandria and in other Mediterranean ports; at the end, these products reached Greece and Italy, where they were used in religious ceremonies, just as for the manufacturing of make-up or of medicines. Other precious goods were gold, silver, glass, orpiment, damasks and silks, the latter imported from remote China. The exorbitant revenues of said trade making them richer and richer, as a result Nabataean merchants were able to unceasingly expand their own sphere of influence along the trade routes, from the Persian Gulf till remote Abyssinia. In this historical stage, the Nabataeans substantially remained nomads, though

they controlled safe localities where they could set up their camps even for very long periods, during the bad season: Hegra, in Saudi Arabia of today, along the track that went from the kingdom of Saba to the Mediterranean Sea, was one of these outposts. Even Petra – that the Nabataeans called Reqem – in that period must have been little more than a vast caravanserai, a protected place where their tents could be arrayed and drinking water was available, thanks to the perennial springs gushing out in that zone. Meanwhile, the Nabataeans found themselves many a time having to confront with the ambitions of two Hellenistic kingdoms, born from the breaking up of Alexander the Great's empire: the Seleucid realm in Syria, and the Ptolemaic one in Egypt. It is a renowned fact that in 321 b.C. the Nabataeans from Petra succeeded in repulsing an attempt to take over their lands by Antigonus I Monophthalmus, one of Alexander's former generals, who was fighting against his former comrades to take over in the region. In fact, they barricaded themselves on the top of the mountainous massif of 'Umm al Biyara, where we can still observe several huge cisterns for collecting rainwater, and the remains of

a shrine, which, perhaps, was erected as a memorial of the event.

Between the III and the I century b.C. the "cultural revolution" took place fostering the rise of the Nabataean kingdom; politically speaking, this became possible thanks to the progressive weakening of the Seleucid kingdom, which was entering into conflict with Roman expansion in the meanwhile. The Nabataeans progressively consolidated their control over the area that went from today's Palestine to the Arab desert, and from the gulf of Aqaba until the borders with today's Syria; meanwhile, they speeded up the process to

12 Left: the Umm al Biyara stronghold, a wholly invincible, natural fortress.

12 Top, right: the remains of a Nabataean shrine built on the summit of Umm al Biyara, on the edge of the precipice.

12 Below, right: the map indicates the borderlines of the Nabataean kingdom at the moment of its foremost expansion (I century A.D.).

13 The wide hollow where the Nabataean capital lay, seen form Umm al Biyara.

attain sedentariness. In the Meantime, their social system evolved from a tribal type of society (where the tribe-chief had to have his power acknowledged by an assembly of his peers) to a monarchy which drew its inspiration and manners from contemporary Hellenistic models. A quotation in the Books of the Maccabees referring to year 168 b.C. approx. - unfortunately the only one of its kind -, cites the name of a king Aretas, who is currently considered the first sovereign of the newly born Nabataean kingdom. His successors began to add an epithet to their own name (e.g., Aretas III was called Philhellene), thus following the Hellenistic sovereigns' model. The evolution of Nabataean society must have been extremely fast; permanent cities were founded (besides Petra and Hegra, also Advat, Mamshit and Shivta, in the Negev), an army was formed, and they even began minting coins. By the I century b.C., their ramified commercial system comprised a series of stable caravan stations, inclusive of temples, thermal plants, barracks and even banking facilities, so that money did not have to be carried for long stretches. However, these fixed settlements preserved their aspect of big

largest port-towns of the Near East (among which Sidon) and of the western Mediterranean Sea (Pozzuoli), besides Rome.

If, at the beginning of the I century b.C., the main antagonist of the Nabataeans was the Hasmonean kingdom of Palestine, quite soon – namely at the arrival of Pompeus's legions, which conquered Syria and Palestine permanently in 64-63 b.C.– the leading opponents to watch out from became the Romans themselves. Kings Obodas II (62-59 b.C.) and Malichos I (59-30 b.C.) had to confront several invasion attempts, and even Petra was besieged. Nabataean sovereigns, however, managed to preserve their substantial autonomy, also thanks to able diplomatic relations and to tribute-paying. It was probably in this period that Petra – due to its strategic position – was chosen as the kingdom's capital. The continual relations with the great commercial – as well as cultural - trends, besides its remarkable economic wealth, made it quite soon a cosmopolitan and artistically dynamic centre, where stylistic contributions from Syria, Egypt and the Hellenized world flew in. Even if the Romans were weakening Nabataean caravan trade - since

encampments, at least until Roman conquest, since only religious, public and representative buildings were built in masonry. In the reign of Aretas III (86-62 b.C.), the Nabataean kingdom reached its foremost territorial extension, managing as it did to control as far as today's territories of Jordan, Negev, Sinai and part of Arabia, until Hegra; stable communities of Nabataean traders settled in the

they had inaugurated a new commercial route along the coast of the Red Sea-, the Nabataeans succeeded in confronting the situation by increasing their own agricultural and mining resources enormously, to such a point that the copper from their mines was exported throughout the Near East; the apogee was attained at the time of the reign of king Aretas IV (8 b.C.-40 A.D.): this was the monarch after whom Petra's most spectacular monument was quite likely named, i.e. el Khazneh (or Khaznet Far'oun), and during whose rule Petra lived through its greatest architectural flourishing. His successors Malichos II (40-70 A.D.) and Rabbel II (70-106 A.D.) kept Rome's expansion at bay with alternate fortune; Rabbel II even went as far as selecting Bosra (in today's southern Syria) as the kingdom's second capital, lest Petra fall. Despite all efforts, this occurred in 106 A.D., when Trajan's legions took over the capital and the realm, probably in a bloodless campaign. To keep on challenging Rome actually would have been tantamount to suicide, and the Nabataeans preferred being absorbed within the empire while

marked its slow but steady decline. Moreover, Trajan had opened up a new road between Bosra and the gulf of Aqaba, excluding Petra from its route. This weakened it fatally, and relegated it to a role as a town of secondary importance. For a couple of centuries the rocky city stubbornly managed to remain an active commercial centre and, at the end of the III century, Diocletian's political reorganisation of the eastern part of the empire brought about its appointment as capital of the province called *Palaestina Tertia*. Meanwhile, having been given the official title of "metropolis", Petra saw its Christian community grow quickly, so much so that it soon became a bishopric; thus, some basilicas were erected in the city, whose floors were decorated with beautiful mosaics in the Byzantine style, and many of the more ancient rocky structures were transformed into churches. Though the city had been struck by two violent earthquakes already in 363 and in 419, life continued calm and the city prospered, even if the original Nabataean population was starting to thin out, due to the increasing migratory waves, above all those from the Arabian peninsula. It was the terrifying earthquake

14 Left: a denarius minted under Trajan to celebrate both Petra's conquest and the establishment of the province of Arabia.

14 Right: the ruins of the so-called "sky-blue chapel" remind us that Petra was the seat of an archbishopric already in the IV century.

15 Left: portrait of Ludwig Burckhardt, who "discovered" Petra in 1812.

15 Right: two celebrated lithographs by David Roberts: a general view of Petra (above) and one of el Deir (below).

maintaining a series of privileged relations. Petra – where the imperial legate took office – was annexed to the Roman province of Arabia and remained a flourishing commercial centre for a few decades. The development of other caravan poles in the north, such as Gerasa and Palmyra, however, as well as the transfer of the administrative powers to Bosra,

in 551 that nearly completely depopulated it, interrupting its slow but steady evolution brusquely. After the Arab conquest of the region in 663, and a further, devastating quake in 747, Petra remained virtually uninhabited and thus began the slow agony of what was left of its magnificent monuments. The city fell into nearly absolute obscurity until the beginning of the XII century, when, for a short period, it was fortified by crusaders, who called it *Li Vaux Moise*, or the "valley of Moses", thus honouring the belief that the biblical patriarch had passed through this area on his long walk from the Sinai toward the Promised Land, guiding the people of Israel. After 1189, the year when even *Li Vaux Moise* was conquered by Saladin, Petra was definitively abandoned and its name forgotten. Only an occasional erudite knew about its existence, but oblivion actually lasted until 1812, the year of the young Swiss explorer and Orientalist Johann Ludwig Burckhardt's visit. Through his perfect knowledge of the Arab language and culture, this man had been able to make himself be taken as a Muslim pilgrim visiting the nearby tomb of Aaron. Thanks to this stratagem, Burckhardt managed to see with his own eyes the incredible rock-cut monuments. Petra then was inhabited only by a few Bedouin tribes which were quite bellicose and always in contrast the one with the other, so that his stay was very short: the fabulous city carved from rock had been rediscovered, however. The news, which spread very quickly throughout the western world, quite

soon attracted new and adventurous visitors, who travelled in the region under the protection of permits issued through the payment of hefty rewards to the various local sheiks. We must remember that all such hostility towards strangers was justified both by the century-old isolation in which the Petra-settled Bedouin tribes had lived in, as well as by the false conviction that, amongst the ruins, incommensurable treasures were hidden, buried by a spectral "pharaoh" (the biblical narrative, distorted

by folk fantasy, had actually transformed the figure of Moses into a sort of a good magician, and his historical rival into the most perfidious and greedy of sorcerers). Among the first visitors were, in 1818, the English Charles Irby and James Mangles, followed ten years later by the French Léon de Laborde and Adolphe Linant de Bellefonds, whose drawings of the main Nabataean rock-cut monuments soon became famous throughout Europe. Indeed, it was the rising fame of Petra - which later the English poet John William Burgon would make immortal by describing it as "rose-red", "half as old as time" -, to attract in 1839 the Scottish painter and drawer David Roberts, who is now considered one of the most talented and influential XIX century landscape painters. The lithographs made out of the drawings executed on location, originally appearing in the ample collection titled *Holy Land* and published between 1842 and 1849, gave him everlasting fame, and are still among the most known depictions of Petra's monuments. Towards the mid XIX century, this wave of romantic explorers, adventurers and artists, was followed by the first credited scholars, who began the systematic exploration of the archaeological area. Amongst them were worthy personages such as the English Austen Henry Layard and Edward Beer (who identified the Nabataean language as a version of Aramaic) and the French Honoré d'Albert and Melchior de Vogüé. It was the Germans Rudolf Ernst Brünnow and Alfred von Domaszewski, however, who carried out the first systematic study of Petra's Nabataean monuments, that they catalogued based upon their position and by giving them a numbering that is still followed and added to today. It is no chance that their work *Die Provincia Arabia*, published between 1904 and 1909, remains a milestone. The events of the XX century involving the whole region, from World War I to both the 1948 Arab-Israeli and the Yom Kippur conflicts, repeatedly interrupted archaeological researches, which have been resumed with renewed impulse only since the early '90s, following the peace signed by Jordan and Israel. To these bear witness the most recent and stirring discoveries in different areas of the city, which foretell what the future of Petra may be.

16 Left: from 1842 till 1849 David Roberts was busy publishing his colossal work, titled Holy Land, in six volumes containing 247 lithographs, 14 of which represent Petra. In this illustration we see the façades of the Palace Tomb and of the Corinthian Tomb.

16 Right and 17: three further suggestive views of Petra: the Tomb of the Obelisks and the Bab el Siq Triclinium (top), the Tomb of the Urn (below) and el Khazneh (opposite).

16

PETRA AND THE NABATAEANS

Though the historical events involving both Petra and the region around it be known, at least in general; it is clear that Nabataean civilisation keeps on defying in-depth analysis, mostly due to lack of written sources. Verified data being unfortunately very scanty and fragmentary, at the moment only archaeological investigation seems able – though quite slowly – to dissipate obscurity. The succession of Nabataean sovereigns has long been determined thanks to the study of epigraphs and coinage. Many other aspects, however - such as religion, daily life, farming techniques -, are known only superficially; we are even unaware as to exactly what area of the Arabic peninsula they came from (so much so that some say they came from Mesopotamia, others from the Persian Gulf region).

It is ascertained, instead, that Nabataeans began settling in Petra's valley toward the end of the IV century b.C.; such a choice was doubtless justified by the strategic position, along two of the main caravan roads of the region, the one from Gaza to the Mediterranean as far down as Hegra and Leuke Kome in the Arabic peninsula; the other, from Alexandria, through the Sinai, venturing north towards Bosra and Damascus. The area, moreover, was easily defended and, above all, it included several perennial springs. The place where the Pink City stands is shaped like an amphitheatre encircled by high, steep walls (which are approximately 3 km away north-south, 5 km away east-west); additionally, the peaks of some of the surrounding reliefs were easily reached should it have been necessary to castle there while fleeing from an enemy. The main access to the valley, moreover, consists in the extremely narrow canyon, the Siq, which can be controlled without any difficulty even by a small garrison. The hollow is crossed by the bed of a nearly always dry torrent, the Wadi Mousa, which, with its tributaries, delimits two low, rocky *plateaus* where the actual city spread out, only to be razed to the ground by earthquakes later. During its first decades, Petra's aspect must have been that of a great and untidy tent camp, whose inhabitants slowly but surely gave up their nomadic vocation and learnt all the techniques required to erect the buildings and the other infrastructures which were necessary to the survival of an ever more populated community. The beginnings must have been quite difficult, because the Nabataeans did not have any traditions of their own in such fields: farmers they were not, nor were they good builders, or planners. In substance, they were compelled to learn everything they needed by observing the people with whom they traded, and by experimenting from time to time. The greatest

18 Rather less awesome than Umm al Biyara, but much easier to get to if necessary, the al Habis stronghold dominated the western area of Petra's valley.

19 Above: the remains of a Nabataean dam, to be seen along the "Little Siq". Similar structures are to be observed in practically every wadi around Petra.

19 Below, left: on the northern flank of Gebel al Khubtha, the straight fissure where the aqueduct passed stands out.

influences they got from the Hellenised world, with which they entertained tight contacts; nevertheless, under many respects, the Nabataeans devised absolutely original solutions. The gravest problem to solve for an ever growing community was water supply: indeed, the springs in the region could ensure only a fraction of their needs. It is a fact that Petra is not located precisely along the caravan routes we mentioned, but a few kilometres away: accordingly, the Gaia settlement– today's Wadi Mousa – was much nearer to said routes and, what is more, water here spouted more abundantly. Petra, however, is set at the bottom of a big hollow, and the Nabataeans imagined that that could solve their problem. Accordingly, they devised an extremely complicated canalisation system carved in the rock, a part whereof was for conveying the spring waters towards the city, while most of it collected rainwater in a extremely widespread manner, carrying it towards ever more capacious conduits, which, in turn, filled enormous rock-cut cisterns, cut and covered with thick layers of waterproof plaster, to prevent evaporation. Thus, during the scarce annual rainfalls, Petra's inhabitants would collect a sizable amount of the rain falling onto an approx. 92 sq km basin! Of course, this required an in-depth study of local geography, that the Nabataeans succeeded in exploiting with extraordinary ability. In fact, the courses of all the seasonal torrents that draw together into Petra's hollow (the Wadi Mousa, but also the Wadi Muthlim, the Wadi an Nasara, the Wadi Farasa and many others) were accurately regimented by

building massive obstructions, which met three requirements. First of all, these dams (often built in sequence along the same wadi) drastically slowed down the crazy rush of the water mass generated by the most violent storms, which otherwise would have carried huge quantities of stones along the valley, thus devastating everything (just think that, as late as 1963, a group of tourists were killed in the Siq by one of these sudden floods). Second, the dams brought forth small - though quite deep- ponds, which would supply other canalisations, prepared for both the supply of drinkable water to the city, and for irrigation purposes. To end with, the obstructions were a good defensive system, above all if near them an outpost - or an observation tower - was erected. In the Small Siq you can still see the remains of one

19 Below, right: this canalisation dug into the rock conveyed rainwater into one of the Umm al Biyara cisterns.

19

of these dams, whose masonry was made of solid blocks of well-squared stone. As time went by, the Nabataeans perfected ever more sophisticated captation and distribution systems, by using earthenware piping, legs of aqueduct built high up (to pass through the valleys and other natural depressions), sluice-gates and decantation basins, to clarify drinkable water. Accordingly, they succeeded in meeting their water needs to such a point as to be even able to build fountains and monumental nymphaea in the city. At the same time, the Nabataeans learnt agricultural techniques and built wide terracings (some are still visible at Wadi Mousa); in a few cases fields were located along the wadis, and were irrigated by making the water overflow at the nearest barrages. There, they probably cultivated cereals, fruit trees and vineyards;

moreover, some areas were used as grazing ground for herds of goats and sheep, other than for the livelihood of dromedaries and horses. In conclusion, the Nabataeans perfected a kind of hydraulic engineering that was in no way inferior to the Roman one.

Petra developed enormously between the I century b.C and the II A.D., when its population swelled to no less than 20,000 inhabitants; nowadays, it is difficult to perceive that at its moment of greatest splendour, between the reigns of Aretas III and Aretas IV, the various urban structures were distributed over an area of about 50 sq. km, within a ray of 6 from the centre, where the Colonnaded Street ran. As a matter of fact, Petra did not appear as a classical Roman or Hellenistic city, arranged along orthogonal road axes: the built-up areas alternated with public buildings and edifices for worship, whilst whole suburbs were scattered around what was the real city centre, sometimes at remarkably varying altitudes. This was due also to the need to preserve from urbanisation the small flat zones that were easier to cultivate, so that, from far above, the city must have looked like a curious patchwork of built-up areas, gardens and cultivated fields. To adequately defend such a metropolis – protected though it was naturally – must not have been an easy undertaking. A continual enceinte would have been too expensive and required a tremendous effort (the remaining sections of curtains still to be seen in the south-west and north-east parts of the city are likely to date from the Roman domination, and the Byzantine period, when, by then, the urban network had dramatically shrunk). With much practical spirit, the Nabataeans preferred placing along the town's perimeter a considerable system of small forts and watchtowers, whose garrisons would warn the population, in case of imminent danger, by means of optical signalling (fires, and use of mirrors). Moreover, all the rock-cut

20 Left: a glimpse of the mansion known as Dorotheos's home; the aqueduct canal may be seen distinctly.

20 Right: a rocky habitation in the outer Siq.

21 Left: a few Nabataean coins, with the effigies of king Aretas IV and queen Shaquilat.

21 Right: a possible likeness of goddess Al Uzza-Aphrodite.

roads were conceived so that they could easily be blocked, whilst the routes for communication that crossed the gorge were defended by posts whose strategic position would have enabled even a small garrison to keep likely attackers in check.

Such complex hydraulic engineering and offensive-defensive equipment meant very high costs, involving, for sure, a State-system that was able to cover them, along with well-organised and stable power structures. Actually, the Nabataeans, who had definitively settled down by now, had set up a hereditary monarchy, based on the models of the nearby Hellenistic kingdoms, that wielded the political-military power and possibly also the religious one, although it was not too much conditioned thereby: indeed, it seems that great rivalry never rose between the priestly caste and the ruling dynasty which, on the contrary, was always very stable. Unusual features for the epoch were the democratic nature of the Nabataean State, and the active, very important, role women played in society – the latter feature being confirmed by a few funerary inscriptions whence we gather that they were fully free to posses land, personal property and collaborators. It is a fact, moreover, that they could even ascend the throne, the names of a few queens having been handed down. Amongst

them stands out the figure of Shaquilat, Rabbel II's mother, and for many years the royal regent. In all cases, the influence in political life of the sovereigns' wives – who used the title of queen -, mustn't have been slight, given that some of their effigies appear on coins next to those of their husbands.

Rare historical documents tell us that civil life was regulated by legislators and magistrates, whose importance must have been inferior only to that of the monarchs' and of the priests'. The pinnacle of the social pyramid was obviously represented by traders, followed by craftsmen and by the military; even sculptors and artists were acknowledged a certain degree of prestige, and it is a renowned fact that many craftsmen handed down their trade from father to son. Then came farmers, shepherds, stonecutters and workmen; slaves were quite common, their life probably being not too hard, and, in many a case, they were considered members of the family.

As for religion, the Nabataeans were polytheists and worshipped gods of pre-Islamic Arab origin: the main deity was Dushara (the god from Shera, the relief dominating Petra's valley from the east), who lived in the mountains and presided over natural phenomena, regulated seasonal cycles, guaranteed fertility to the soil and the living and, finally, looked after the royal dynasty. Also worshipped were al Kutba, patron of writing and foretelling, besides a female triad, of whom Al-Uzza "the mighty" was the goddess *par excellence* -the other two being Allat and Manawat-, lady of life and of love. These gods were not anthropomorphous and, as a result, Nabataean religious culture was aniconic: deities were not depicted as human figures, but by means of betyles, i.e. simple geometric shapes (cubes, parallelepipeds, etc.) symbols not of the god, so much so of its presence. As time went by, the Nabataean pantheon absorbed also deities of their Syrian and Edomite neighbours, such as Atargatis (lady of harvests) and Ba'alshamin. The encounter with the Graeco-Roman civilisation brought about

the progressive assimilation of local deities with foreign ones: Dushara was identified once with Dionysus, another time with Zeus-Jupiter; Al-Uzza with Aphrodite-Venus, al Kutba with Hermes-Mercury, Allat with Athena-Minerva, Manawat with Nemesis. Al-Uzza, moreover, was also assimilated with the Egyptian goddess Isis, whose divine prerogatives she shared. The contact with the western world fostered also an iconographic revolution, so much so that next to betyles in the I century A.D. also figurative representations of the various gods appeared. Unfortunately most of these

were destroyed by Islamic iconoclasts, who, in pursuance of the edict of caliph Yazid II (720-724), cancelled nearly all human depictions in Muslim lands.

Through the various gods of their pantheon, the Nabataeans worshipped nature's primeval forces, especially water, and light in its multifarious manifestations (the Sun, the Moon, Venus). This explains the existence of several "high places of sacrifice" around Petra – arranged as a sort of mystic crown on the biggest reliefs (Gebel Attuf to the south, Gebel Umm al Biyara to the west, Gebel ed Deir to the north-west, Gebel al Khubtha to the east), evidently to protect the city and its inhabitants – and of rock shrines near springs or water courses (as in the Wadi Siyyagh or in the Wadi Muthlim). The "high

places of sacrifice" are open-air shrines that can be reached along daring processional roads cut into the rock, which priests and the faithful walked up periodically to offer their gods the blood of sacrificial victims (mainly lambs and little goats), but also bloodless offers such as cereals and other commodities. They usually seem to be oriented based upon evident astronomic references (especially, the "movement" of the Sun), but this specific aspect has been given scarce attention by scholars hitherto. In any case, it is quite symptomatic that god Dushara was related to the Sun, as two goddesses were to the Moon (Allat) and to Venus (Al-Uzza), thus forming a luminous triad.

For sure, the Nabataeans, believing in some sort of life after death, also thought that the souls of the deceased became supernatural entities which, somehow, kept on looking after the world of the living. That explains the ardour with which they dug extremely extensive necropolises all around their city and why, next to their tombs, tricliniar chambers were always arranged, where family meetings and banquets honouring ancestors took place.

What still has to be understood is the aspect of the city of the living. It is very likely that Petra's hollow was taken up by a monumental unit, whose pole was the street that ran along the well-regimented course of the Wadi Mousa, surrounded by living quarters and suburbs farther away. The houses of the ordinary folk must have been simple, one- or two-storeyed, squared buildings, built of stone and bricks cooked in the sun, with a flat roof, whitewashed and plastered, and with their windows usually facing inner courtyards, rich in green, if possible. Arrayed as they were the one next to the other, these habitations left little room for a network of alleys arranged according to the outline of the ground, and very narrow, to ensure as much shade as possible. Since wood was not plentiful in the region, structural elements such as beams, frames, doors and windows had to be used over and over again. Moreover, inner chambers were no wider than about 3 m, due to the small size of the beams used for coverings. All together, Petra mustn't have been all that different from an old Jordanian village. Also, during the hottest months, people would perhaps sleep in tents laid out on the flat roofs.

These stretches of small houses were interposed with cultivated areas and orchards, whilst here and there rose the large masses of public and religious buildings. Other dwellings - various ambiences connected by staircases and terraces - were carved into the rock of the wadis surrounding the city. Fresh and comfortable, they boasted walls and ceilings embellished with polychrome paintings showing the influence of the style of both the Hellenistic and Roman worlds: architectural wings, false doors, or more fanciful creations such as fake pergolas and flourishing gardens. As demonstrated by the excavations currently under way (2006) in the "district" known as ez-Zantur (behind the Great Temple), in the I century b.C. they already lived in sumptuous houses, whose beauty was even mentioned by Strabo. These included numerous and spacious rooms devoted to social and organised relationships, according to the Hellenistic-Roman style, around peristyles and colonnaded vestibules. Said ambiences, provided with stone floors, were stuccoed and profusely painted with rich polychromies; the less taken-care-of residential part of the house, instead, was arranged irregularly, according to the eastern habit.

Temples and public edifices, such as the Qasr el Bint or the Temple of the Winged Lions, were built lofty with the stone that was unceasingly extracted from the quarries around the city; though they showed traces of Hellenistic influence first and of the Roman one later, these monuments exhibited wholly original, structural and decorative features. The Qasr el Bint itself, with its square layout and the three contiguous *cellae*, declares the substantial autonomy that local builders achieved with regard to classical

23 Above: the Nabataeans are likely to have begun carving their first rocky structures already during the III century b.C.; Petra's urban development, however, started only in the I century b.C..

23 Below: in the area known as ez Zantur, the excavations of a large house belonging to the I century A.D. are under way; the ruins of another house (see photograph) can be seen nearby.

canons. The Nabataeans were like sponges ready to absorb all ideas from the peoples they came into contact with. Thus, in Petra's big buildings, Syrian, Egyptian, Greek and Roman elements freely flew in together, and were conjugated through unheard of solutions, among which is the massive employment of the so-called Nabataean - or "horned"- capital, i.e., a local invention. It is also evident – for instance, in the façade of the Palace Tomb – that the "golden proportion" amongst the various parts, common to Greek and Roman house building, was granted little attention over here. Also the sculptural decoration of these edifices reflected said situation: the Nabataeans, as we have already said, did not possess a figurative tradition of their own and, starting at least from the end of the I century b.C., studios of sculptors, modellers and artists who had trained abroad - if not even foreign ones -must have been active in the city.

Along its perimeter, the town of the living slowly but surely got mixed up with the town of the dead; such unusual combination, which is quite difficult for us to understand, must have been second nature, instead, to Nabataeans, because of their religious beliefs as to the hereafter. Nowadays, given that practically nothing at all remains of the city proper, visitors' attention focuses on the necropolises, where several hundred - bigger or smaller, and elaborate - tombs stand out (currently, no less than 3,000 items have been catalogued at Petra, from sepulchres to simple, dug-into-the rock betyles). Some of them are extraordinary art pieces, even though many, albeit fascinating, if compared to contemporary Greek or Roman masterpieces are quite more modest. The kinds of styles are rather heterogeneous, and several scholars believe that each one represents a different cultural influx, other than a different historical period. Others, instead, believe that the various architectural models do not correspond at all to a chronological sequence, and were all employed at the same time over at least three centuries' span (which seems logical, given also the few tombs that may be ascribed to the more "recent" styles). For practical purposes, however, the various architectural styles have been classified according to types.

The first burials, which can be ascribed to the IV-III century b.C., are the **ditch tombs,** i.e., simple rectangular chambers carved into the rock; of a little later are the **well tombs**, meaning hypogeous chambers, to be reached through a sort of chimney. Very similar are the **dromos tombs**, where the well was substituted with a corridor leading to the burial chamber. In the II century b.C. the **Assyrian style tombs** began to spread, whose simple, smooth façade is topped by one or two rows of step-like merlons, imported as a matter of fact from Syria; the door can be set between pilaster strips and topped with a simple entablature. Meanwhile, a type of capital based upon the classical Corinthian style evolved. Very simplified however, it is called "horned" or Nabataean, and was widely used in the cavetto **tombs**, where the façade is surmounted by a showy curvilinear cornice similar to the cavetto, on which only two, enormous step-like merlons rest (that is why they are also called staircase tombs). Moreover, the front is enclosed within pilaster strips bearing Nabataean capitals, whilst the door is

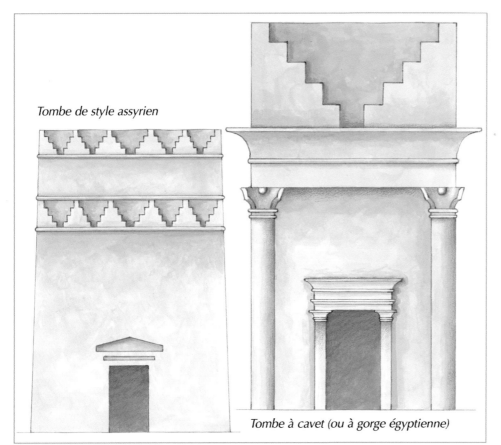

Tombe de style assyrien

Tombe à cavet (ou à gorge égyptienne)

24 Right: the Tomb with the Split Pediment (above) is an elegant example of the classic Nabataean style, whereas the Tomb of the Roman Soldier (below) is a perfect instance of pediment tomb.

enriched with a more or less complex entablature. An elaboration of this model is given by the **double cornice tomb**, where, beneath the cavetto cornice, a classical type cornice is inserted. The attic included between the two cornices may be emphasised by short pilasters with Nabataean capitals, whilst the door is usually surmounted by a gabled pediment with acroteria. Since the second half of the I century b.C., architectural and decorative motifs coming from the Hellenistic world had been by then adopted in Nabataean architectural lexicon, thus giving rise to the **classical Nabataean style tombs**, of which el Khazneh is the most superb example. By seeking ever more exaggerated mightiness, the size of tombs became colossal, and innovative solutions were introduced – such as the superimposed orders of columns and the employment of the *tholos* – side to side with by then obsolete elements (such as rosettes or animals depicted in a heraldic fashion), thus denoting the provincial character – quite original though it was – of Nabataean architecture. An example of these are, besides the Treasure, the Tomb with the Split Pediment, the Renaissance Tomb, the Bab el Siq Triclinium, the Corinthian Tomb, Sextius Florentinus's Tomb. Dating from after Trajan's conquest in 106 A.D. are, to end with, a few rare tombs with pediment (meaning, similar to the façade of a tetrastyle Roman temple) which may be ascribed to the **classical Roman style**: the Roman Soldier's Tomb and the quite similar wadi al Najr tomb, besides few other badly preserved examples. The Palace Tomb and el Deir, which may be classified as classical Nabataean style, because of the difficulties linked to their dating and function remain unique.

Even the so-called **arc tombs**, whose door is surmounted by a simple curvilinear gable or tympanum, are quite problem-rousing: according to some scholars, they are of the same epoch of the Assyrian and cavetto ones, according to others they might be ascribed to Roman domination.

To end with, some practical considerations. Petra's rock-carved tombs may give the impression of being an incredible waste of resources and energy. However, to carve a room or a façade into soft sandstone, under many respects is much less tiring and expensive than erecting a building, also because walls and ceilings stay up by themselves. The study of the so called Unfinished Tomb (p. 95) has allowed us to understand that the carving work proceeded from the top downwards. With the help of wooden scaffolding, but above all thanks to mobile platforms, upheld and manoeuvrable through a complex play

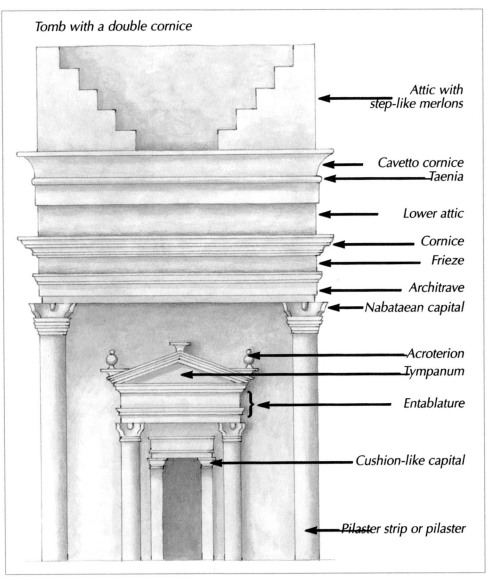

Tomb with a double cornice

Attic with step-like merlons

Cavetto cornice

Taenia

Lower attic

Cornice

Frieze

Architrave

Nabataean capital

Acroterion

Tympanum

Entablature

Cushion-like capital

Pilaster strip or pilaster

of ropes, workmen first had to square out the rocky surface with pickaxes, chisels and stone-saws. On this flat surface, subdivided into squares thanks to plumb-lines and strings, the general design of the architectural details was outlined, which were eventually carved and sculptured in relief in the rocky mass; every element would then be smoothed and finished off, besides carving for the funerary chamber or the inner, hypogeous rooms. Since soft sandstone did not usually allow to execute minute decorative details, in several cases (especially above the portals), some mouldings in harder stone were embedded in appropriate grooves which could eventually be carved to produce finer details. In a few cases we know of the use of plaster on façades (more common, instead, in inner chambers), but, as of today, it seems that the theory whereby façades were mostly stuccoed and painted, is groundless. Among other things, it is evident that, after processing, rich sandstone polychromy wanes in time, perhaps because of oxidation phenomena; marblings, in fact, stand out where the rock has been eroded more. This must have made the aspect of façades more uniform compared with what they look like today.

To conclude, Petra's rocky structures are "work converted into stone", laboriousness fixed into the rock as an admonition for commitment, and a testimony of exquisite craftsmanship and sensibility: that is why they deserve all our admiration and attention, so that they may be preserved as long as possible.

26 Left: throughout Petra, a few tombs of the utterly atypical, and quite difficult to date, "arc" type, are to be seen. In the opinion of some scholars, they belong to the I century b.C., according to others they are to be dated from after the Roman conquest.

26 Above, right: the wonderful tholos of el Khazneh - the monument that, justly so, is considered the classic Nabataean style masterpiece, that has recently been attributed to the middle of the I century A.D.

USEFUL INFORMATION

FOREWORD

The visit to the ancient Nabataean capital has been divided into five main itineraries, which require no less than two days at one's disposal. Considering the distances existing between the main monuments, the myriad smaller rocky structures and the natural beauty of the place, the ideal stay is of four to five days, during which you will also be able to undertake the remaining tours.

Each path is marked with one to four asterisks, indicating the level of difficulty (*and** are suitable for everybody; ***and**** are recommended only to expert walkers).

As a suggestion, bear in mind that from the gate entrance to the el Khazneh archaeological area, the descent of el Siq requires about 30 ', as many as you need to reach the Museum. From here to el Deir –whose visit is a must – you have to allow 3/4 of an hour's walking. Travelling time from one point of interest to the other, therefore, is anything but insignificant.

With an entry fee, the visit is possible from 6 a.m. until sunset (generally, at 5 p.m.); you get a daily ticket, but you may buy a discounted one valid for three days. Groups also benefit from considerable reductions in price.

THE BEST TIME TO GO.
MEANS OF TRANSPORTATION

You may visit Petra all year round, but winter is rainy, quite cold (8-13°C) and there are less daylight hours. In case of a snowstorm, undoubtedly rare - a pity it is not foreseeable -, the dead city changes into a fairy-like place. At the peak of summer, on the contrary, weather is, to say little, torrid (it can far exceed 40°C), but at least the locality is practically desert and at your

27 The area where Petra's ruins stand is extremely large: also in the deep side-valleys, you will meet with considerably interesting tombs and rocky structures. It is better, however, not to walk too far away from the paths. The three tombs here, on the left, are to be found in the wild wadi Ma'aiserat, whilst the enigmatic Monument of the Serpent and the nearby tower-tomb (here, above), rise in the wadi Thughra, an hour's walk from Petra's centre.

28 As shown by the images, Petra's rocks are full of even quite exposed hypogea, passages and stairways, that often end over the void. Do not venture along these itineraries, therefore!

29 Petra's whole, extremely extensive archaeological area, unfailingly rewards visitors with wholly unexpected as well as fascinating "discoveries": this tomb, whose heavily eroded façade displays a fabulous chromatic range, is to be found near the Tomb of the Urn.

complete disposal. Definitely, the seasons best indicated to visit the rose-red city are spring (15-25°C) and autumn (16-23°C). The best months are April and May, also because oleander bushes are in full bloom, and that, in itself, is a priceless show. To avoid crowds – and the hottest hours – we recommend to begin the visit when the sun is dawning and, after a long pause to recover your strength, to continue in the late afternoon.

Near the access gate to the archaeological area, you can rent a colt, a donkey, a dromedary or a carriage (always accompanied by a guide, though), with which to descend el Siq as far as el Khazneh (with the carriages), or reach the New Museum (on the back of an animal). We therefore suggest you ask before paying for the service. Also close to the New Museum, in an area called Nazzal's Camp, you can rent a mount to climb to el Deir or to el Gebel Attuf (prices are cheap and the guides competent).

If you are tourists used to getting off on your own, Petra is a magnificent place, where, by complying with a few basic rules, you will breathe the air of adventure in complete safety: the archaeological area is really vast and it is not rare to have a monument at your own exclusive disposal also for a few hours (el Deir above all). Moreover, the whole area is constantly patrolled by an efficient tourist police corps, which you can trust without hesitation. If instead you prefer to be accompanied, in the village of Wadi Mousa, and also near access gates or hotel receptions, it is easy to find the addresses of qualified tour guides: generally, they are reliable and prices are reasonable.

SOME FURTHER ADVICE

To fully appreciate your visit to Petra a few simple precautions are required. The one applying to all the year regards footwear: if you do not want to spoil either your day or your feet, give up clogs, beach sandals, any type of light shoe or with a smooth sole. Walking for hours and hours on the gravel, or climbing up rather steep paths, carved into the live rock, without adequate footwear, rapidly becomes torture, made more annoying by the sand that penetrates everywhere, and by the shrubs, that are generally quite prickly. If you want to be comfortable: wear light boots, or high, closed, heel less shoes, and with rubber soles: the so-called burlap "amphibians" are ideal.

Clothing is also important. Do not let either the generally torrid weather, the magnificent sun or the frequently blowing breeze fool you: avoid going round too bare, because getting a sunburn or even a quite serious sunstroke among these rocks is all but difficult. Therefore, do not forget to have with you headgear, sunglasses and plenty of sun cream. Scanty female (also male) clothes, moreover, can cause some embarrassment, and it is not in fact

polite to irritate the sensibility of the local people or of the warders, whose politeness is actually proverbial. On the whole: no one will criticize your clothes, but it is not the case to go round in a bathing suit, given that a pair of shorts and a t-shirt are much more practical, above all in view of the fact that Petra is not a beach.

At the beginning of spring, it will be useful to bring with you a light sweat shirt or, anyhow, some long-sleeved clothing, since sudden climatic changes are not infrequent and, after a heavy shower, the temperature in the shade can drop suddenly several degrees. It seldom rains in Petra and usually in the spring months: waterproof clothing is not really indispensable, as it is easy to find shelter anywhere, without saying that after each shower both wind and sun will dry your clothes in a few minutes. A basic element for a comfortable visit to Petra is water: dehydration, here, is not to be underestimated, it can cause unpleasant moments. Remember that, because of the continuing breeze, your skin might seem dry, but that does not alter the fact that it is perspiring profusely. Therefore, be sure always to take with you at least a litre of water (we recommend you buy a handy plastic bottle at one of the kiosks at the entrance to the site; remember not to leave it lying around) and to regularly drink a little, above all if you are in the midst of a laborious ascent.

If possible, do not remain in the direct sun more than is necessary, and during the hottest hours avoid moving round too much: eat something light and nutritious (fruit is ideal), and rest in anticipation of a long afternoon full of delight. Do not drink alcoholic beverages – beer is also excluded!- because in a hot and dry climate they are harmful.

SAFETY RULES

Having at one's disposal a few extra days, we strongly recommend visiting Wadi Siyyagh, Wadi Mataha and "Little Petra" (El-Barid), three remarkable locations above all for the exceptional pleasantness of their landscape. However, we must emphasize that these excursions – especially the first two – are recommended only to expert walkers, and on days that are not too hot.

From an excursionist's point of view, for trekking enthusiasts Petra is an authentic paradise, in virtue of the kilometres and kilometres of paths and stairs carved in the rock: always changeable, the scenery is -to say the least – extraordinary, and offers unrepeatable subjects to photography lovers. Some passages lead you to breathtaking panoramic points, where you can admire all the main monuments from privileged, absolutely astonishing angles. In these pages, it is not possible to provide a full picture of such itineraries and, besides, each one of you will easily find the most suitable path through your own ability. Nevertheless, we recommend maximum caution: do not abandon the well-trodden paths if you are not used to the mountain or to long, demanding walks, as frivolous imprudence could generate the gravest consequences. Many ancient communication paths are eroded and in bad condition, others end abruptly without warning (literally, on precipices that make your head spin), others disappear among rocky expanses where orientation becomes quite arduous: to this we add barrenness of the place and the temperatures, that also in the most favourable periods are subject to sudden rises.

ENCOUNTERS AT PETRA

Up to present, some Bedouin families belonging to the Bedoul tribe still live in Petra's archaeological area: these are the current inhabitants of the rose-red city. In reality, the government has built modern homes for them close to Wadi Mousa but, in spite of this, some seem to prefer the traditional ways of life. Generally, they occupy groups of rock tombs adequate to their needs and guarded by vigilant dogs; you can meet them in the Wadi Mataha and in the Wadi Farasa, but also elsewhere. They live on sheep farming and modest trade, they are proud, reserved, polite and - the elderly - still vaguely xenophobe. Their children are nice, and in no way annoying, the women are often occupied in traditional activities. You will be aware of their presence also at a distance from the lines of clothes, hanging outside the openings of the tombs. Respect their privacy and their culture:

this is their home and, before having a look around and taking photographs, think of how you would feel if you found a group of tourists in your living room, speaking an incomprehensible language and wanting to immortalize you at all costs. However, be trustful: the Bedouins – also donkey and dromedary steerers: do not forget this is their job! – are honest, loyal, trustworthy people, and gifted with a strong sense of dignity. Do not offend them with inappropriate behaviour. If you are able to establish a good human contact, they will gladly show you some well-kept secrets of the Nabataean capital.

A much more unusual and rare encounter, but not impossible, is that with a really particular reptile: we are talking about a kind of big lizard, whose peculiarity lies in its unlikely colour. The "Agama sinaita" – or Sinai lizard – is in fact of a beautiful brilliant blue, the function being sexual allure. No longer than 30 cm - its very thin tail included -, this elegant saurian is harmless; if frightened, it rapidly changes colour to camouflage itself with the surrounding environment. It turns greenish-brown starting from its tail, and the head is last to remain blue, with a really surreal effect. If you happen to meet one of these odd Petra dwellers, you'll have to be real quick with your camera if you want to immortalize it in its showiest livery; in any case, you will know that it was not a vision due to too much sun. Finally, you could bump into another big lizard, but be informed that these reptiles are harmless. Instead, be careful where you put your hands, especially in dark and humid places along less oft-trodden paths: scorpions and big spiders are quite rare, but however present.

SOUVENIRS AND MEMENTOS

Petra being a tourist location, as a result you will find souvenir sellers just about everywhere, at Wadi Mousa, also along el Siq, the colonnaded street, or the steep path for el Deir. The most typical local handcrafted products are glass bottles, skilfully filled with multicoloured sand, usually gathered on site (this is a small example of the unbelievable multitude of colours that nature has given to this place), silver jewellery and reproductions of antique Nabaetean manufactured articles. We wish to emphasize this concept, because it is good to know that even the less cheap-looking souvenirs are nearly always modern replicas – ranging from terracotta oil lamps to coins – and in no case should you overpay them.

30 Behind the gaze of Petra's current dwellers- at times apparently severe, sometimes smiling- is hidden the lofty and friendly soul of the Bedouins, most of which belong to the ancient Bdoul tribe. If their assistance as guides is extremely precious, their honesty is proverbial.

31 The Agama Sinaita is one of Petra's most striking inhabitants. Since this lizard is quite shy, it is much easier to stumble upon it in the least-trodden zones. Throughout the archaeological area, you will much more often find other big, wholly innocuous lizards, though their aspect be threatening.

Among much junk, some Bedouin women or boys will offer you authentic objects, generally Nabataean or Roman coins, but it is well to know that the export of archaeological findings is strictly prohibited by the Jordanian government.

You will notice, moreover, that the ground near the tombs is - without exaggeration - littered with pottery fragments: to pick up some as a souvenir is tolerated, but digging in the sand to take home intact objects is not. Before filling your pockets with fragments, in any case, think of what a sad life they will have on your desk, or on a library shelf, covered with dust and out of their context. All things considered, it is better to look but not to touch. Finally, absolutely respect the sacredness of this unique place: do not litter, do not damage the monuments, do not shout unnecessarily: to appreciate the mysterious fascination of Petra better, you must know how to listen to its silence.

ITINERARY 1 - THE SIQ *

Of course, the visit to Petra begins from the entrance-gate to the archaeological area: it can be interesting, however, to spend a few words on today's built-up area at Wadi Mousa. This chaotic agglomeration of snow-white edifices probably stands on an ancient Edomite settlement – the bygone Gaia – which in the IV century b.C. became a considerably important Nabataean centre, and perhaps even the local sovereigns' residence before the transfer of the court to Petra. In the high section of the village, just in front of the entry to the urban agglomeration and opposite a modern fountain, the interior of a little white building similar to a mosque preserves the perennial spring (Ain Mousa: Mousa is the Arabian word for Moses) which, according to Biblical tradition (Exodus, 17. 1-7) was made to spout by Moses with the touch of his stick, to quench the thirst of the people of Israel marching towards the Promised Land. The presence of the source itself was the main reason for the settlement's

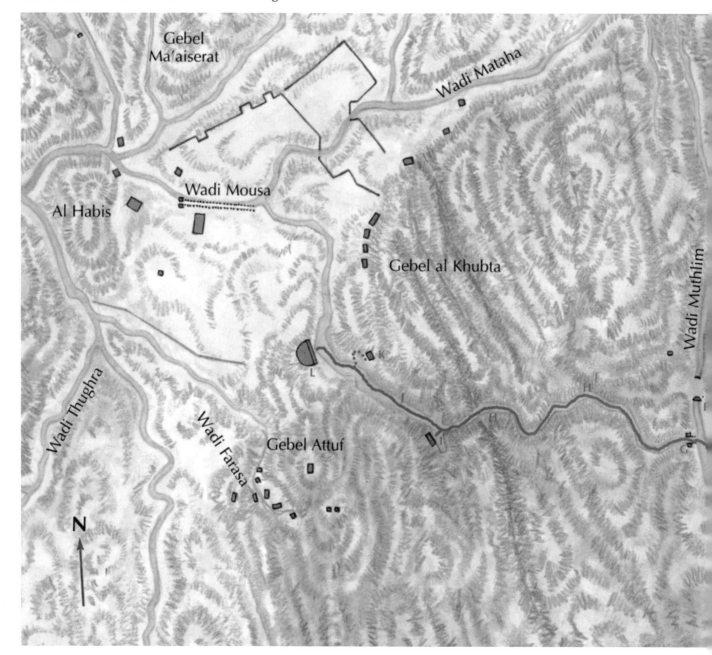

existence; when Petra developed into an autonomous centre, the flow of the spring was regimented in a canalisation and conveyed to the rocky city along the walls of the deep gorge currently known as the Siq. Inside today's built-up area and in its immediate surroundings you can still observe several rock tombs (once a part of the local necropolis), a few cisterns and, above all, what remains of the terracings shaped by the Nabataeans for farming purposes. Near Wadi Mousa, moreover, you can visit the archaeological excavations of the Edomite site called Tawilan. To end with, right next to the entrance-gate, included within the precinct of the luxurious Petra Forum Rest House (Petra Forum Hotel), you can observe a beautiful, big tomb,

33 Left: Still today, from the rock that Moses touched according to tradition, a perennial flow of clear water keeps on gushing out.

33 Right: now turned into a kind of luxurious bar, the tomb known as al Khan is considerably interesting due to the portico it displays opposite the façade, sculpted into the live rock.

A Wadi Mousa
B Entrance gate
C Tomb of the Serpent
D Djinn Blocks
E Tomb of the Obelisks
   and Bab el Siq
   Triclinium
F Nabataean tunnel
G Entrance arc
H Inner Siq
I El Khazneh (the
   "Treasury")
J Outer Siq
K Uneishu's Tomb
L Theatre

nowadays used as a bar; known as al Khan, what mainly makes it interesting is the colonnade preceding it on the two sides, dug into the live rock. Nearby, there are also some ruined kilns for cooking ceramics, and an enormous cistern (al Birka), where the water of Moses's spring was collected, before it continued its flow toward Petra.

Even before beginning your walk, you had better stop and contemplate for a second the whole valley around you; it is evident that all the rainwater –rare though it be- falling in this extremely extensive area, flows into the bed of the seasonal torrent known as Wadi Mousa, flanked by the easy unpaved road where every day tourists swarm by.

It seems impossible that such a scrubby, sometimes completely dry rivulet, may change in a few seconds into a roaring, even many-metre-high mass of water, during the most furious storms, but this is really the kind of trouble that the Nabataeans, as we shall see, had to cope with and alleviate.

A few hundreds of metres from the entrance, there where you start to see the first rock tombs, on the right-hand side stand out three curious monuments whose shape is unmistakeable: they are the so called **Djinn Blocks**, which were obtained from the core of the rocky mass by excavating a candid emergence of sandstone. The three enigmatic blocks, which the Bedouins once thought were the dwellings of cruel spirits (the Djinn, in fact) able to scare to death anybody that bumped into them, are likely to date from the I century b.C., and probably were tombs. Of the three monolithic cubes, from 6 to 9 m high, two are undecorated, whilst each of three sides of the third are decorated with four pilasters; it is clear that the plinths, the capitals and the cornices must have been made with another kind of harder stone (you can still see some fragments *in situ*), embedded within the live rock and eventually snatched by some marauder or merely torn down by one of the many earthquakes that upset the region in the past. The hypothesis that they be tombs is said to be confirmed by the small ambiences excavated in the two small blocks and by the loculus dug, instead, on the summit of the larger cube; the sloped surface dug into the wall at the back, therefore, probably served for lifting the sarcophagus, which was eventually placed into the rectangular cavity through a gangway. However, we must underline that, according to some scholars, the Djinn Blocks are, instead, godly simulacra, sacred to Dushara (indeed, often depicted as a cube) and placed to protect the pathway, as well as the entrance to Petra. According to others, the name Djinn (viz., "spirit") reminds us of their function as receptacles of the warden spirits of the Nabataean city. To end with, we must remember that their other Arab name – Sahrij (or Sahreej) – means "water reservoir"; this interpretation might seem utterly unacceptable, yet, in the area of Petra, we are to find another 23 similar monoliths, all curiously placed right near either a watercourse, a spring or a big cistern. Since, in this case, behind them, you can clearly notice the horizontal fissure dug into the rock, where the aqueduct once passed, it would not seem unlikely to think that the Djinn were the dwellings – namely, the containers – of the spirits in charge of protecting what was the Nabataeans' most precious resource: water.

Right in front of the Djinn Blocks, on the opposite side of the Wadi, you can see a curious sandstone emergence, rounded off by erosion and before which, nowadays, there is a short stairway: this is the **Tomb of the Serpent**, whose tiny entrance leads to a funerary chamber in whose floor 12 loculi open; on one of the walls you notice a bas-relief which seems to depict two serpents intent on attacking a four-footed animal, while, not too far way, another

34 Left: the carving of the three djinn blocks required tremendous toil, since the monoliths were dug out of the bulk of a rocky ridge. Behind, and below, them, you will be able to notice the groove where the aqueduct passed.

34 Right: the high relief sculpted in the Tomb of the Serpent, depicting a horse with a strange object on its back, may not belong to the Nabataean period at all: while it is likely to be the work of some Bedouin, its meaning remains an enigma.

graffito represents a horse carrying a cube (?) on its back. The meaning of such a depiction is a mystery, even if the figure of the snake, for the Nabataeans, was linked with the heavenly world, which it guarded.

A few metres beyond this, Petra's first two monumental structures show off, placed one above the other, so much so that, at first, the group would seem to be a single architectural unit. The upper one is known as the **Tomb of the Obelisks**, whose name clearly comes from the four, originally 4-metre-high, obelisks, surmounting the upper part. Probably of Egyptian origin, and of an absolutely unique kind at Petra, they actually should be just as many *nefesh*, meaning aniconic depictions of the souls of the

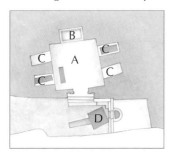

Plan of the Tomb of the Obelisks

A Funerary chamber
B Arcosolium loculus
C Loculi
D Well -tomb

back, shaped as an arcosolium; a well-like tomb unfolds in the terrace before the façade.

Right under the monument we have just described, but not perfectly in axis therewith, is the so-called **Bab el Siq Triclinium**, which is not a burial but, as its name indicates, a tricliniar room whose purpose was to house the banquets and symposia that took place periodically to honour the deceased. In fact, in the completely bare interiors, the triclinium benches– running all along three sides of the rectangular hall -have been preserved well. Due to its position which is very close to the bed of the Wadi Mousa, unfortunately the monument appears to be much more eroded than the tomb above. The elaborate, emphasised façade – whose succession of pilasters,

35 View of the Tomb of the Obelisks and of the underlying Bab el Siq Triclinium. As for the likely interpretation of the four obelisks, we must also remember the opinion according to which they are supposed to be mazeboths, *a Biblical term indicating a godly simulacrum, or image: the function of the four monoliths, therefore, would have been to protect both road and travellers. This would equalize them to the two obelisks on the Gebel Attuf.*

deceased. The relief dug into the wall rising behind the obelisks, inside a niche surmounted by a Doric, Nabataean frieze (namely, one where the triglyphs alternate with simple paterae, or slightly relieved discs) represents a standing male personage, dressed according to Hellenistic fashion; according to a few, this is supposed to be a fifth deceased person, whose body was put into the tomb at a later stage. The drastic change in the figurative style of the monument might be justified by the different building dates of the two burials. Dating the tomb, however, remains a problem, despite the presence, on the opposite side of the wadi, of a double inscription in Nabataean and Greek, quoting the burial of a certain «Abdmank, son of Akayus, son of Shullay, son of 'Utaih», who lived at the time of king Malichos: should the epigraph really refer to the Tomb of the Obelisks (a datum which is controversial), there remains the fact that two sovereigns named Malichos reigned at Petra, one in 59-30 b.C., the other in 40-70 A.D.. However, the employment of Greek demonstrates nevertheless that Petra was already a cosmopolitan city between the I century b.C. and the following one. In all cases, the interior of the hypogeum, that you reach by passing through a door surmounted once again by a Doric Nabataean frieze, includes four loculi dug into the side walls, and a fifth one, in the wall at the

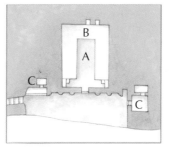

Plan of Bab el Siq Triclinium

A chamber
B triclinium bench
C service rooms
    (or funerary chambers)

35

curvilinear pediment above the door and upper-placed semi-pediments recall that of the Corinthian Tomb (see p. 49) – might indicate that it is of a later date compared with the Tomb of the Obelisks: nowadays, while the latter is usually thought to date from the first half of the I century A.D., the *triclinium* is believed to belong to the second half. At Petra nothing is ever really certain and, as a result, whilst some believe that the tricliniar room was built as the outfit of the sepulchre above it, others think that the tombs relating to the *triclinium* are the two cavities opening on the sides of the façade. The only certain datum is the translation of the name: Bab el Siq, as a matter of fact, means "the door of the Siq". Here one realises that the valley where the Wadi Mousa extends, is a colossal funnel, which shrinks progressively until it conveys all rain towards an immense sandstone bank, against which all the kinetic energy of the seasonal water masses discharged during millennia, thus opening up a road for them in a fissure, perhaps caused by a shattering seismic shock, which thus originated the real – or inner - Siq. Before you enter

into the shady canyon, it is worthwhile noticing some further details. The course of the Wadi Mousa, spanned by a reinforced concrete bridge, appears here to be blocked by a dam (dating from 1991), conveying the sudden floods rightward towards an impressive, 100-metre-long furrow in the mountain side, that suddenly changes into a real **tunnel**. Both the bridge and the bank substitute similar structures that had already been built toward the ending of the I century b.C. by Nabataean engineers, who also constructed the new course of the torrent and the 86 m long tunnel. The Nabataeans, in fact, to prevent the flood waves from continually flowing into the gorge, which was one of the leading entrances to the city, thus provoking recurrent destruction, compelled the water course within the contiguous Wadi Muthlim, also known as the Little Siq; thus the waters of the Wadi Mousa deviated lengthily around the Gebel al Khubtha massif, and eventually returned, appeased, into the ancient river bed in Petra's hollow, right at the beginning of the Colonnaded Street. Near the mouth of the tunnel, a djinn block

36 Above, left: one of the piers, sculpted into the rock, which is what is left of the large monumental arc placed at the beginning of the Siq.

36 Above, right: the narrow mouth of the Siq, with the ruins of the arc.

36 Below: the Nabataean tunnel, deviating the waters of the wadi Mousa and the nearby djinn block.

is quite evident, decorated with a round of Assyrian crowsteps: its presence would seem to confirm the link between this kind of monument and water courses. Opposite the dam, on the rock, six small obelisks (or *nefesh*) are sculpted: one of them bears an inscription giving Petra's Nabataean name: Reqem. Once it has crossed the bridge, the unpaved road suddenly becomes a sheer slope and enters dramatically into the **inner Siq**, a spectacular ravine, about 1 1/2 km long and embedded between walls that are from 90 to 180 m high, and in some points no more than 3 m the one from the other. The access to this natural marvel is marked by the remains of an awesome arc, whose (albeit) worn-out piers sculptured in the rock you can still see; the two niches originally must have housed just as many statues. We do not know when this monumental door was built – perhaps originally it might be barred by two, heavy wooden panels – ; yet, based upon evident Graeco-Roman influence, it is said to date from the second half of the I century A.D.; the arc, instead, appearing in a lithograph by David Roberts, and whose scant remains are to be seen to the left high up, collapsed in either 1896 or the year before.

Here, as well as long the whole way, you will notice just as many deep furrows in the two flanks of the ravine: they are the Petra-bound canalisations which conveyed the water of the fount of Moses and of the other springs spouting in the surroundings, and crossed the bed of the Wadi Mousa in conduits embedded in the Nabataean bridge. The aqueduct to the north (namely on your right) seems to be the oldest, and the fluid probably flowed uncovered in it for a long time; the one to the south, is likely to date from to the period (first half of the I century A.D.) when the bottom of the gorge was regulated with a constant and stone-paved slant. Remains of the

original flooring – uncovered between 1997 and 1998 – are visible in several points. At a later stage, the water of the two canalisations was made to pass through piping of conduits made of cylindrical terracotta pieces (some still in place), joined together with much mortar; this contrivance limited dispersion, while increasing pressure at the same time. Along the Siq, moreover, numerous inscriptions in Nabataean and Greek are to be

37 Left: a glimpse of the Siq, with the grooves of the two aqueducts.

37 Above, right: in 1998, while excavations were under way to uncover the original Siq flooring, a statuesque group was unearthed – quite eroded in its upper part -, whose size was bigger than the natural dimension, depicting two tradesmen descending the ravine, followed by just as many dromedaries. A little on, another similar group may be spotted, yet oriented in the opposite direction.

37 Centre, right: about half way through the Siq, a sandstone emergence stands out of which, on its side facing the valley, displays a nice niche. Inside it, there are two flanked betyles, the one smooth, the other displaying markedly stylized facial features - eyes and a nose-, that are thought to represent goddess Al Uzza.

37 Below, right: the manifold betyles and the votive niches to be seen along the Siq are the testimony of the devoutness of the Nabataean merchants arriving at - or leaving- Petra.

found, besides about fifty betyles and votive niches, and a sculptured group discovered in 1998. Some natural widenings in the canyon must have served as caravanserais, meaning as stations for the caravans that, through Petra, went to and fro the Mediterranean and Arabia, as well as Syria and Egypt; in these points, along the rocky walls, you can observe some man-made chambers, perhaps guard-posts or "offices" of the excise-men.

In a spot where the Siq becomes darker and bends rightwards, appears suddenly the wonderful façade of **El Khazneh** (the Treasury), Petra's most famous rocky building. The charming beauty of this monument and its scenographic position leave you utterly breathless. The colossal façade was dug into the rocky wall facing the narrow opening of the

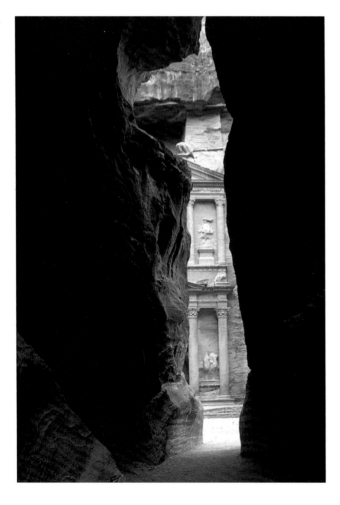

inner Siq in a natural widening, there where the canyon (Wadi al Jarra) brusquely bends rightwards; one's astonishment is increased by the nearly perfect state of the monument, which even amazed the first European visitors, such as Léon de Laborde, Charles Irby, James Mangles, David Roberts, who all shared the conviction that they were standing before an

unmatched structure the world over. The monument's sizes are remarkable – m 39.6 (height) by 28 (width) – but the withdrawn position of the façade related to the natural profile of the vertical wall emphasises its majestic features (and has ensured its protection from atmospheric forces throughout the centuries). The lower part of the monument consists in a portico with a pediment, whose six columns with Corinthian capitals are 12.5 m high; despite their aspect, only the two central ones (the one on the left was restored in the early 1960s) are free, whilst the other ones lean onto the mass behind. In the two external intercolumniations, two equestrian groups are sculpted featuring Jupiter's twins, Castor and Pollux, unfortunately quite worn out, just like the other ten relief-sculptured human figures which decorated the upper part. This is due to the destructive action of the iconoclasts who, abiding by the edict of caliph Yazid II (720-724), obeyed the order to destroy all human depictions to be found in the lands of Islam. The long frieze running along the colonnade consists in racemes and volutes alternated with vases placed between gryphons (or griffins) turned toward each another; the tympanum, at whose centre stood a Gorgon head, displays an elegant decoration with volutes. At the extremities of the overlooking attic-whose upper part is provided with a continual row of rosettes-, two lions (or sphinxes) serve as acroteria. The second storey is divided into three elements: at the centre is the *tholos,* namely a small round temple, with its conical roof topped by a large Corinthian capital bearing an urn, also damaged.

This element gave the Arab name to the rocky edifice – Khaznet Far' oun, namely the "Pharaoh's Treasure" – due to an ancient belief, according to which Moses's ghostly pharaoh enemy (who, in the dark ages following the collapse of classical culture became, in Bedouin fantasy, a sort of wicked sorcerer endowed with supernatural powers) concealed immense riches therein. By trying to lay their hands on them, generations of Bedouins aimed at the urn with their rifles, in the attempt to break it and make the treasure fall to the ground. The alto-relievo female figure sculptured in the central intercolumniation of the *tholos,* is likely to be an effigy of Tyche (Destiny, but also Fortune), since she holds a cornucopia in her left hand and a patera in the right. However, it is interesting to note that the acroterium placed at the apex of the pediment – and therefore at the goddess's feet – is formed by a solar disc set between two spikes of wheat and two bovine horns: such symbolism, typical of Egyptian iconography, is linked with goddess Isis, and therefore the mysterious figure is believed to be more correctly identified with Isis, assimilated with both Tyche and the Nabataean goddess Al Uzza. The other two bas-reliefs to be found on the sides of the *tholos* can still be recognised as Amazons brandishing axes, similarly to those placed in the intercolumniations of the two semi-pediments; finally, the figures placed in the niches between the semi-pediments and the *tholos* are two winged Nikes. The continual entablature running above the capitals of the upper storey is decorated with a frieze bearing leaf garlands and acorns, whilst four, very worn-out, gigantic eagles serve as acroteria.

38 In the half-light of the Siq, the sudden appearance of el Khazneh rouses unforgettable emotion.

39 Left: the two showy sequences of holes bored on both the sides of the façade have provoked unending queries. They may be stairs (similar to those visible on the fronts of many quarries), but even wooden scaffolding anchorage. The fact that they terminate at many metres from the ground can be explained, instead, by taking into account that the rocky rubble produced during the carving work, as time went by, formed a pile at the foot of the monument being prepared. When the digging (carried out from the top downwards) reached that mass of inert material, the Nabataean workmen no longer needed stairs or scaffolding, but only had to stand on the debris, being made fall down into the valley gradually, and eventually removed from the site.

39 Right: detail of one of the Corinthian capitals.

The interior of el Khazneh includes a large vestibule (or pronaos), wherefrom eight steps lead up to the main hall, a 12 m-sided cubic chamber onto which three smaller ambiences open; the sole decorations consist in the elegant, pediment-like door jambs. Other two smaller rooms, also preceded by a stairway, look onto the two short sides of the vestibule.

The date and the function of el Khazneh have been

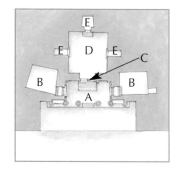

Plan of el Khazneh
A vestibule (or pronaos)
B side-rooms
C lustral (or holy) basin
D large hall
E niches

40 Above, left: the side of the big cubic chamber – the main ambience of el Khazneh-, measures 12 m.

40 Below, left: also two minor ambiences open up onto the vestibule, which were illuminated with elegant oculus-shaped, big windows. The underlying portals are quite smartly decorated as high reliefs.

40 Right: a foreshortening of the recently discovered tombs at the foot of el Khazneh, inside which human remains were found, together with part of a rich outfit. The deceased's DNA was obtained from the bony material, that is now being studied. Starting from the skull, a team of Copenhagen's medicine university managed to reconstruct the physiognomy of the noble Nabataean.

the subject of much controversy ever since its discovery; some thought it was a temple, some a royal sepulchre, some said it dated from the realm of king Aretas III (86-62 b.C.), some even to the period of emperor Hadrian (117-138 A.D.). Archaeological excavations carried out starting in 2003 (and still under way in 2006) however, have solved the enigma. First of all, we must think that the original level of the square facing the monument was about 6/7 m lower; sand and stones were deposited there over the centuries by the water course, once the Nabataean dam placed at the mouth of the Siq had collapsed. In the rock wall facing the gorge, four tombs with a pediment-like façade were excavated at first; the objects discovered inside them (including some bony fragments) let us understand that they were the burials of very high-ranking personages – a sovereign and his relatives, in all likelihood – which have been dated as first decades of the I century b.C. As a result, it should be the sepulchre of king Aretas IV (8 b.C.-40 A.D.). Since a monumental staircase was spotted in front of the three façades, conceived in such a manner as not to damage the burials (they even went as far as to open up a skilful window on the side to brighten accesses to the tombs), clearly the rocky edifice to be reached along this stairway - namely el Khazneh, was built at a later stage. Moreover, it has been ascertained that the access to the tombs was guaranteed by building a staircase on the left side, whose opening was at the level of the terrace dug into the sandstone, and opening just in front of the façade of el Khazneh. All this leads to a sole conclusion: the superb el Khazneh is the funerary temple consecrated to the worship and memory of king Aretas IV, and its accomplishment – which took place shortly after the sovereign's death – must belong to a period falling between 40 and 60 A.D.. The little purification basin dug into the threshold of the large hall (apt for receiving the blood of sacrificial victims) seems to confirm the worshipping function of the monument.

Today we still have to understand whether the matchless rocky building was the work of hands that had come from the Hellenised world (probably from Alexandria), or of Nabataeam craftsmen, nevertheless trained in a Hellenistic environment.

From the esplanade onto which el Khazneh looks, the gorge bends right, northbound, and – once it has taken the name of **outer Siq** – it begins its descent towards the hollow where once Petra stood. Among the various rocky structures jutting before your eyes along the walk, is the big square cavity unfolding high up, on the right-side wall, that was originally a

façade of Tomb 69 is emphasised by four pilasters. The most interesting, however, is Tomb 70, which juts out very much related to the rocky wall and is topped on the three sides by (Assyrian) crowsteps, whose kind is absolutely unique. In front of this group of sepulchres stand other six tombs, side to side: the most interesting are 825 and 826 (the two northern-most), since their façade is furrowed by the groove of an aqueduct; initially, the cutting that

41 Left: a glimpse of the outer Siq; from the left to the right-hand side you will recognize the façades of tombs nos. 67, 68, 69, 70 and 71.

41 Above, right: one of the large tombs looking onto the right-hand side of the outer Siq.

41 Below, right: the unmistakable Tomb no. 70, topped by step-like merlons of the Assyrian type.

wide tricliniar chamber; in the rock sculpted just a little above the upper edge of the chamber is sculptured a curious (and quite rare) human, stylized figure, whose meaning is obscure. Nearly in front of the *triclinium* you will notice the remains of Tomb 66 (according to Brünnow's classification), whose base, sculptured with circles and lozenges, remains. It collapsed in 1847, and incorporated a long Greek inscription commemorating the defunct, a twenty-seven-year-old named Arrianus, who died of a disease "that wins everything". Just a little further on, to the left, five mighty contiguous tombs stand the one after the other (nos. 67, 68, 69, 70, 71); Tomb 67 will be noticed due to its unusual funerary chamber placed between two step-like merlons, whilst the housed the earthenware piping was sealed with mortar, and painted in such a way as to hide its presence. In a higher and slightly withdrawn position related to the rocky outline, on the left, you will notice a nice façade of the double-cornice type: it is Tomb 813, better known as **Uneishu's Tomb** from a fragment of inscription found nearby, wherein is quoted «Uneishu, brother of Shaquilat, queen of the Nabataeans». This woman was the wife of Aretas IV and the mother of Rabbel II, during whose childhood she reigned for six years; this permitted to date the sepulchre from the years 70-76 A.D.. We must note that the term "brother" is here understood to be a synonym of prime minister. The tomb was preceded by a porticoed court, whereupon opened also a tricliniar room; inside, along the walls of the funerary chamber, as many as thirteen loculi open, an indication that the sepulchre was used by the relatives of the governor for a few decades, according to a respected tradition.

From the court placed in front of the tomb, your eye will wander over the underlying outer Siq, whose original level was 2 or 3 m lower compared with today (the paved road must have run along a canalisation that collected the rainwater coming from the deep lateral valleys); the western wall of the valley appears to be literally covered with the dark openings of dozens and dozens of tombs, placed at several levels in such a manner as to deserve the definition that already the first western travellers gave it, i.e., of **Road of the Façades**. Such alignments of rocky structures, connected the one with the other by stairways and narrow walkways, are truly a compendium of the most widespread architectural types to be found at Petra, from the Assyrian style tombs to the arc-type ones. The presence of such a vast necropolis right along the main thoroughfare leading to a built-up area may amaze the modern visitor, but was wholly usual in the ancient world, in the areas Hellenistic as well as

42 Left: the Streets of the Façades are veritable compendia of the various architectural styles to be seen at Petra; such a mixture seems to confirm the hypothesis that such diverse models were being used at the same time, and that this occurred for several centuries.

42 Right: Uneishu's Tomb is of the double cornice type, with its portal surmounted by an elegant pediment.

43 The theatre is likely to have been destroyed by the 363 earthquake, but it is also probable that, for some time, it hadn't been hosting shows anymore.

Roman. The peculiar combination of the city of the living with that of the dead is stressed a little further on by the presence of both a few rocky dwellings and the enormous hollow of the **Theatre**, sculptured into live rock along the western versant of the outer Siq, thus further demonstrating the considerable technical and geometrical know-how of the Nabataean craftsmen. Though the overall structure of the *cavea*, divided into three horizontal sectors, and the arrangement of the *orchestra*, consisting in a perfect semicircle, suggest that the monument belongs to the age of Roman domination, it appears to be by now ascertained that this show-house was founded during the kingdom of Aretas IV (8 b.C. - 40 A.D.), modified during the reign of his successor, Malichos II, and eventually enlarged after Trajan's conquest. The especially Roman aspect of the monument is credited to these last interventions; such widening, extending as it did to the whole upper part of the *cavea*, is believed to be the reason for cutting into some pre-existing tombs, whose funerary chambers thus came to incongruously look out onto the wall at the back (it is likely, however, that said cavities were originally concealed with masonry work, which eventually collapsed). The *cavea* consists in 45 rows of seats (only at the ends integrated with sections built in masonry) subdivided amongst three *moeniana* and into six vertical sections by short stairways. A complicated draining system – now restored and working – allows for the outflow of rainwater. Also the surface of the *orchestra* was obtained by digging into the rock, while the stage, facing which is a 38 m long *pulpitum* (a low wall with niches), as well as the scenery building at the back were erected from their foundations as lofty edifices and, as a result, they were torn down by earthquakes and floods; today their well-restored remains are still to be seen, letting us imagine that, as usual, in the scenery wall, three portals opened up, framed between colonnades placed on two storeys. At the sides of the stage you will notice two vaulted passages (*parodoi*), which permitted access to the *orchestra* and the *cavea* through corridors and staircases. In the *cavea*, whose acoustics is exceptional, about 6,000 spectators could sit. Due to the position of the theatre inside the necropolis, it is likely that here, besides tragedies and comedies, holy plays and religious celebrations would be staged, about which, however, we know nothing.

44 Above, left: the Silk Tomb, with its unmistakeable polychrome marbling.

44 Above, right: the extremely worn out façade of the Corinthian Tomb.

44 Centre: panoramic view of the tombs sculptured at the foot of Gebel al Khubtha.

44 Below: the so-called Palace Tomb.

A El Khazneh
B Uneishu's Tomb
C The Theatre
D The Tomb of the Urn
E The Silk Tomb
F The Corinthian Tomb
G The Palace Tomb
H Sextius Florentinus's
    Tomb

ITINERARY II: THE ROYAL TOMBS *

In reality, while in no inscription, nor in any other historical document, are we to find the modern definition of Royal Tombs (which, as we shall see, is erroneous in at least one case), the unheard-of size of these structures – and the costs that their constructing must have involved – are suggestive of an attribution which is probably not far-fetched.

You need an hour, or little more, to complete this itinerary, which begins at the outer Siq, just a little beyond the Theatre. On the right-hand side of the unpaved road heading towards Petra's lower section, behind the refreshments kiosk, a modern stairway climbs towards the rocky wall of Gebel Al Khubtha, here literally 'pockmarked' with hypogeous chambers. Whoever has any extra time to spend, can turn right and walk through the numerous rocky structures standing out in this vast necropolis. The others should follow the steps till they reach the awesome **Tomb of the Urn**, which is easily recognizable due to its massive arched sub-

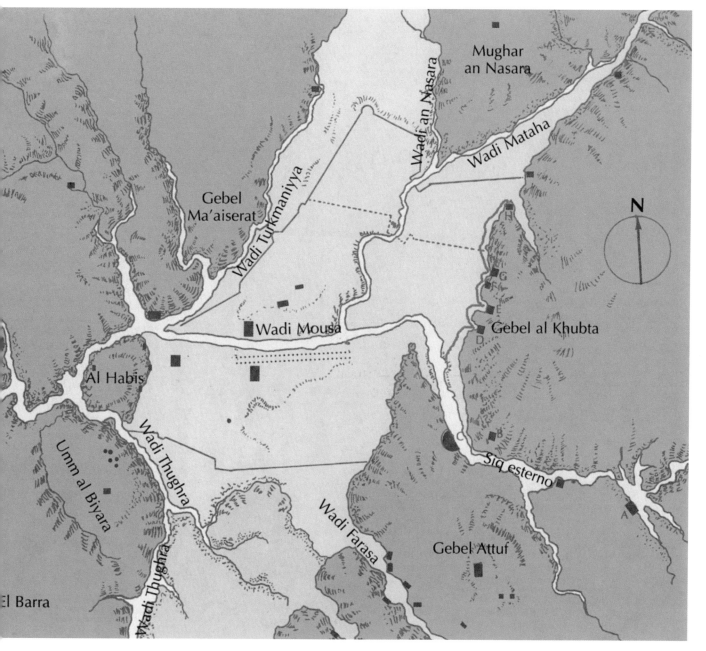

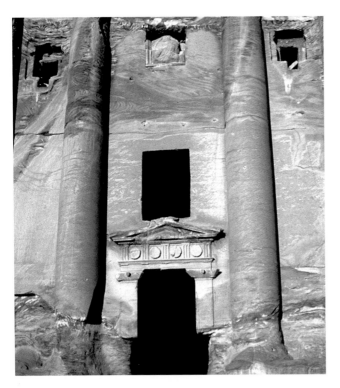

structures facing the colonnaded yard. The tomb –for some strange reason deriving its name from the small (and insignificant) urn acting as an acroterium - has a façade which is very much withdrawn related to the natural mountainous outline. The big, rock-carved court (21.5 m wide), had on its short sides two porticos carved out of the rock; whilst one has preserved its monolithic columns, the other one by now lacks them completely. The esplanade was extended toward the valley by erecting a massive platform (much bigger than the court) consisting of series of vaulted rooms, placed on two storeys and partly collapsed, so much so that it is impossible to say whether these structures supported a third colonnade or not. The façade, of the pediment type, dashing in its sheer verticality, on its sides is set within two smart angular pillars onto which lean column quarters: two high pilaster strips on a podium frame the great portal, topped by the classical Doric Nabataean frieze and by a low pediment. The big window above the entrance was

hollowed out at a later stage, in 447, when the tomb was converted into a Christian church. In the three intercolumniations, many metres away from the ground, there are just as many loculi; only the central one has preserved its closure slab, decorated with a relief bust of a male personage clad in a toga, nowadays very damaged and which perhaps reproduced the features of the burial's owner. According to the most credited theories, this was king Malichos II (40-70 A.D.) and the two lateral tombs, originally also closed with busts, must have been those of his closest of kin, perhaps his wives. The high tripartite attic – whose lower architrave lets us still imagine the presence, in correspondence with the underlying capitals, of four relief busts, perhaps the effigies of just as many deities – supports a pediment whose tympanum is undecorated.

The large inner room (m. 19 by 17), lacking any ornament, on the wall at the end exhibits a wide arcosolium niche, carved at a later stage by uniting

Plan of the
Tomb of the Urn

A substructures
B court
C porticoes
D large room or triclinium
E arcosolium
F niches

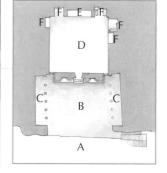

two older niches: in Byzantine times this is where the altar was placed, and the floor still bears the holes bored for the small pilasters which, according to the oriental church's custom, supported the balustrade. Originally, this room was a tricliniar hall, where banquets honouring the deceased took place, but once the transformation into a church occurred, the benches were torn down and the floor was levelled off, whilst two lateral doors were

46 Above: the portal of the Tomb of the Urn is surmounted by a Doric-Nabataean style frieze.

46 Below: originally, the arc-shaped substructure opposite the Tomb of the Urn might have supported a colonnaded portico.

47 Left: the portico on the east side still has its five grooveless columns. The upper loculi were built sometime after the tomb.

47 Right: a glimpse of a fascinating view, near the Tomb of the Urn.

47

hollowed out in the façade.

To the left of the urn tomb, the small façade of the so-called **Silk Tomb** is quite evident. This is unquestionably one of the favourite subjects for photographers, due to its spectacular colouring, which erosion has made even more vivid. The variegations of the sandstone here exhibit a superb range of nuances, going from ochre to saffron yellow, to sky-blue. Besides its showy polychromy,

the tomb is interesting also for a few architectural features. The façade is of the double cornice type, with its inferior part highlighted by four pilaster strips topped by Nabataean capitals; in the external intercolumniations two niches were carved, which curiously enough present just as many relief figures, today no longer interpretable, unfortunately. The attic, surmounted by two step-like merlons, is divided into several sections by three cornices, and

48 Left: the Silk Tomb stands out due to the myriad nuances colouring the fine façade sandstone that inspired poets and writers over the centuries.

48 Right: the Silk Tomb, also known as the Rainbow Tomb, is of the double cornice type, with its attic emphasized by four short pilaster strips.

49 Left: the upper order of the Corinthian Tomb, with the tholos placed between two high semi-pediments, shows a clear influence of the Hellenistic architecture, that had already inspired the building of el Khazneh.

49 Right: the Corinthian Tomb- unfortunately rather impaired by atmospheric elements-, displays marked stylistic incongruousness: the two portals placed between the intercolumniations on the left, especially, spoil the symmetry of the façade.

is portioned out by short pilaster strips in axis with the underlying ones.

Next to the Silk Tomb is the mighty, though gravely damaged, **Corinthian Tomb**. Though it has endured the wear and tear of time very much – carved as it was in a position which is especially exposed to winds and rain – it still is a monument of great architectural interest. It got its name at the beginning of the 1800s from the English travellers

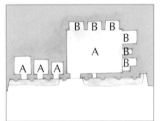

Plan of the Corinthian Tomb

A funerary chambers
B loculi

Irby and Mangles (according to others, from the French Léon de Laborde, in 1828), who defined as Corinthian the floral style of the capitals, similar as they are to those of el Khazneh, though less elaborate. The size of the monument is awesome, since its measures m. 24.5 (width) by approx. 28 (height). The lower part of the façade – emphasised by eight pilaster strips, with the larger portal surmounted by a curvilinear pediment, the upper pediment being split, the repetition in the attic of the horizontal lines of the cornices and of the vertical ones of the short pilaster strips – reminds us considerably of the Bab el Siq Triclinium (p. 35), whilst the upper part – with the central *tholos* and the two lateral semi-pediments – was clearly derived from el Khazneh, of which the Corinthian Tomb is often erroneously deemed a "bad copy". In reality, though it is quite eclectic, this structure represents a curious attempt to mediate between the Nabataean style proper and the elements imported to Petra from the Hellenistic world. The effect may

seem redundant and not well achieved, but such a negative opinion is surely corroborated by the bad state of conservation of the rocky building. The interior, consisting of a main room into which several loculi and three secondary chambers - curiously provided with just as many entrances - open up, must have been the last abode of a high-ranking personage and of his relatives. Until recently, this was considered the tomb of king Aretas III the Philhellene (86-62 b.C.), but the current date attributed to el Khazneh seems to dispel this thesis. If in fact the Corinthian Tomb is a later structure than the Treasure, erected to commemorate Aretas IV (8 b.C.-40 A.D.), chronological attribution must be post-dated at least to the second half of the I century A.D.; therefore, if the Urn Tomb is really the sepulchre of Malichos II (40-70 d.C.), then the Corinthian Tomb should have housed the mortal remains of the last Nabataean sovereign, Rabbel II (70-106 A.D.). Indeed, the monument enjoyed a privileged position, since it was practically in line with the Colonnaded Street (p. 55) and, thus, seen from the city, it must have

been a remarkable scenographical wing.

Right next to the Corinthian Tomb, to the left, rises the gigantic façade of the so-called **Palace Tomb**, which, though lacking the entire upper part, is still the most monumental one at Petra, with its 49 m width and a height of more than 45 m. The structure, whose formal complexity is extreme, is so called because once it was believed to imitate the architecture of the great Hellenistic or Roman palaces (somebody even suggested that it was influenced by the *Domus Neroniana*, the sumptuous royal palace that Nero had himself built in Rome). The only ascertained datum is that its aspect resembles no other rocky Nabataean edifice and that, therefore, it is a unique structure; however, its unusual shape and peculiar position, dominating over the whole hollow once taken up by Petra's built-up area, can help us imagine what its real function was.

First of all, you will notice the fact that, before the façade, comes a sort of a vast platform, more elevated if compared with the ground level; from

50

50-51 It is quite evident how utterly singular the proportions of the so-called "Palace Tomb" are, making it, as they do, resemble, if anything, a theatre's front-stage. This is thought to be a sort of building erected for representative purposes,

whence the sovereign or the royal family showed up, perhaps on special occasions.

51 Right: the pediments of the large doors clearly draw on the Hellenistic tradition.

this terrace, four staircases carved into sandstone led to mighty portals framed between pilaster strips, which in turn were set within semi-pillars with a column quarter leaning on it, topped by large Nabataean capitals leaning on which are majestic tympanums, the two more external ones being curvilinear, triangular the other two. The four enormous, practically bare, inner chambers (only the two central ones communicating the one with the other), bear no loculi, nor do they suggest that sarcophagi were present in ancient times. The

Plan of the
Palace Tomb

A terrace
B halls

second storey leans on an unusual, continual, wholly smooth entablature, and creates an effect of disconcerting contrast: the eighteen pilaster strips, divided into couples, are not at all in line with the vertical ones of the underlying storey. This sort of blind gallery supports a double, frieze-less entablature, now jutting out, now re-entrant, on which a third storey – or attic - leant, highlighted by short pilasters with Nabataean capitals being the extension of the underlying pilaster strips, and divided horizontally into several sections by various cornices. Only the right-hand side section of the third storey was carved out of rock whilst the rest was built in masonry; unfortunately, the earthquakes tore down most of it. Today it is difficult to imagine that the façade continued vertically for still many metres: indeed, on the third storey a fourth one leant (only a small surviving part can be seen high up, to the right), constituted by a continual straight gallery supported by real columns in line with the pilaster strips of the second storey.

Moreover, the showy cut of the mountainous wall, always high up to the right, makes us suppose that it was effected to leave room for a fifth, wholly-built-in-elevation storey, similar to the fourth and concluded by a split, topping entablature. In conclusion, contrarily to its modern looks, the façade was originally prominent for its sheer verticality (reaching a height of about 60 m) and must have been visible from every corner of the city. The overall aspect recalled that of the stage fronts of Roman theatres (think of the still well preserved ones at Merida or Sabratha, in Libya) and appeared

much more balanced than it does today.
Whereas traditionally the impressive monument was thought to be the tomb of the last Nabataean monarch, Rabbel II (70-106 A.D.), the new hypothesis that is making its way suggests that, rather than a sepulchre, it is an edifice built for representation purposes: perhaps the royal palace of a sovereign or, anyhow, a structure linked to royal prerogatives. Some archaeologists – and the author of these lines – think that the balcony placed before the front was a sort of real stage, and that celebrative plays could be performed here or, even,

that the king would appear in front of the public on special occurrences, according to a pompous, oriental-like protocol. The elevated position of the monument and its mighty appearance would have been the ideal scenario for public events of this kind. There remains the problem of the date: had the edifice been devised for a monarch – indeed, perhaps Rabbel II – it would date, anyhow, from before Roman conquest, which occurred in 106. The influence of Roman architecture on the monument does not invalidate the hypothesis, since the Nabataean kingdom had tight relations with the Romanised world already during the I century b.C. The so-called Palace Tomb is the last of the Royal Tombs proper, but it is worthwhile to make a little, last effort, and to go on for a few hundreds of metres; then, turn into the well visible path that, to the left of the monument we just described, heads for the Wadi Mataha, flanking the wall of the Gebel al Khubtha and going beyond the layout of the Byzantine walls. Soon, you shall reach a fork; the side-street on the right indicates the beginning of the steep processional way leading to the top of the massif, the one on the left, instead, leads down to the **Tomb of Sextius Florentinus**, whose façade, carved out at the end of a long and low, rocky

offshoot, faces north-west, and is therefore visible only at the very last moment. Though it is quite worn out by weather, it still maintains an harmonious elegance and, there where the sandstone is most eroded, reveals a spectacular natural polychromy. The front, which is very elaborate, though dating from the Roman period, is anyway considered a masterpiece of Nabataean architecture. The lower order, emphasised by four pilaster strips bearing a continual entablature, displays a nice portal surmounted by a tympanum with pediment; the upper order is dominated by a curvilinear pediment whose tympanum is decorated with a very much eroded Gorgon head, but similar to the one you can see on the façade of el Khazneh. An imperial Roman eagle acts as acroterium, whilst the attic is divided into several sections by two cornices and four short pilaster strips, with Nabataean capitals. The whole thing is topped by a low, triangular pediment, on whose summit leans a little acroterium shaped as un urn. A now scarcely visible inscription engraved in the lower entablature, tells us that this is the tomb of Titus Aninius Sextius Florentinus, Hadrian's legate and pro-praetor of the province of Arabia, who died at Petra in 129 or in 130. Inside the funerary chamber there are five loculi in the wall at the end, whilst other three can be seen in the right-hand side wall. In front of the tomb opens up a square court carved in stone, which originally may have been surrounded by a portico, as is perhaps suggested by a few column drums still to be seen on location.

From here it is worthwhile going back toward the Palace Tomb; who wishes to deepen the exploration of this area can, instead, advance along the Wadi Mataha (see itinerary described on p. 100).

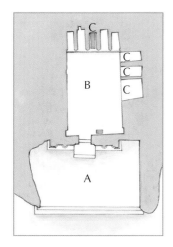

Plan of the Tomb of Sextius Florentinus

A court
B funerary chamber
C loculi

52 Left: further details of the "Palace Tomb". The presence of seven niches in the intercolumniations on the second floor is unexplained; according to some authors, they housed just as many inscriptions, sculpted out of slabs either of harder stone, or of metal.

52 Right: the lively polychromatism enlivening Sextius Florentinus's tomb.

53 The composite style of the tomb of Sextius Florentinus denounces architectural influences that are Hellenistic and typically Nabataean, rather than Roman.

ITINERARY III - THE URBAN AREA*

Just a little after the Theatre, with on your right side the impending Gebel Al Khubta massif - on whose base the Royal Tombs (p. 45) are sculptured-, the unpaved road decidedly turns to the left, there where the outer Siq finally widens into the hollow where the Nabataean chief town stood. Here the ancient bed of the Wadi Mousa meets with that of the Wadi Mataha, where the Nabataeans had conveyed the waters deviated through the tunnel opened at the mouth of the inner Siq. Before going on, we should let our imagination run, close our eyes and pretend that the valley is covered by an expanse of white-plastered, low and flat-roofed houses. Such thick, and messy urban fabric as well, interrupted by kitchen-gardens, orchards and gardens, was - here and there - overhung by the awesome stonework of both the temples and the large public buildings. Inhabited by about 30,000 people, the real city extended until the al Habis stronghold, while the suburbs occupied the non-

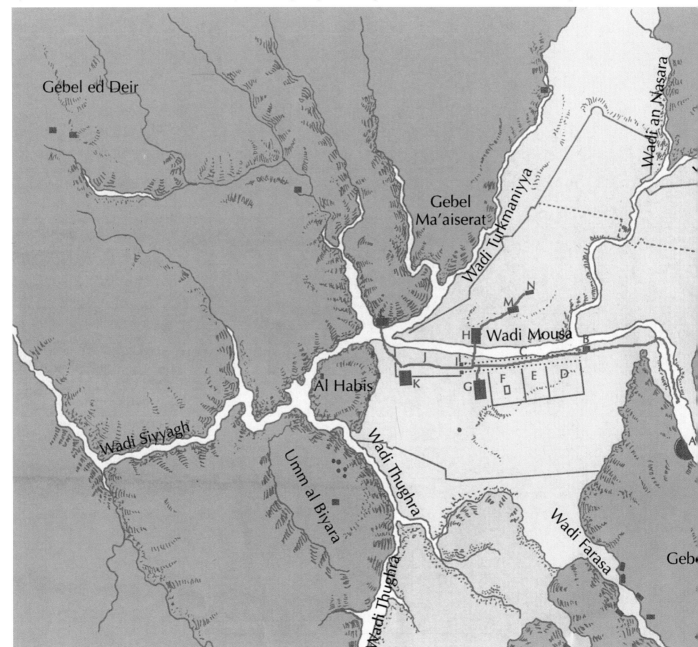

cultivated areas of the surrounding, deep valleys. Nowadays it seems unthinkable that there could be so many edifices, but it suffices for us to tour the low hills surrounding the Colonnaded Street to be aware that we are actually treading over a stretch of unexplored ruins. North-west and southward, the city was protected by two enceintes, that are still at least partly visible; though some scholars stick to the idea that they belong to the I century b.C., it now seems more likely that Petra -as related by Strabo, the historian -, lacked walls at least as late as the first decades of the II century A.D., if not until after the 363 A.D. earthquake.

The Wadi Mousa bed, descending gradually westward enclosed between what remains of the high masonry banks built by the Nabataeans, was flanked by Petra's main, wholly-paved street; this approx. 300-m-long artery received its initial monumental layout probably during the reign of Aretas IV. Though once it probably extended also eastward, it now begins near a **nymphaeum**, whose remains are still well visible next to a solitary tree. This monumental fountain, perhaps decorated with marble stone and statues, was quite likely to be fed by the aqueduct arriving from the Siq. For certain, its presence roused the admiration of whoever arrived from the arid, desert areas of the region, but even more amazing must have been the **Colonnaded Street**, along which were lined up all of Petra's main public buildings and, presumably, a

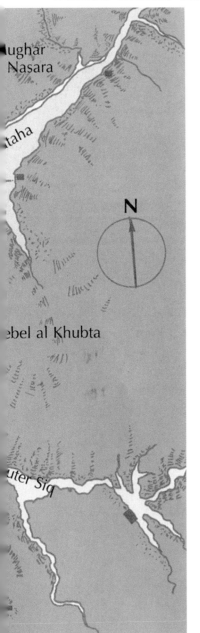

A The Theatre
B The Nymphaeum
C The Colonnaded Street
D The "Upper market"
E The "Central market"
F the "Lower market" (large pool)
G The large temple
H The Temple of the Winged Lions
I The door of the Temenos
J Temenos
K Qasr el Bint
L The Museum
M The Byzantine Basilica
N The Sky-blue chapel

55 Above: a glimpse of the colonnaded street, namely Petra's main artery. Wholly paved, it was flanked on both sides by colonnaded porticoes under which were shops, offices and public houses. The columns were raised again by the Department of Antiquities in 1960.

55 Below: the Temple of the Winged Lions (whose interior features a large number of columns, very close the one to the other) and, in the background, the awesome remains of the "large temple".

certain number of shops, offices and refreshment facilities. Under the shade of the porticoes flanking the street on both sides, business negotiations were carried out, currencies were exchanged, meals were served and talks took place on the latest events. Though archaeological evidence demonstrates that the street was thoroughly modified after Trajan's conquest in 106 A.D., it is still uncertain who - Aretas IV or the Romans - had the flooring laid out and the colonnades erected.

On the left side of the Colonnaded Street, three extensive, fenced-in areas unfolded, at the present time hardly readable and full of rubble, commonly defined – from east to west – upper market, central market and lower market. Archaeological prospecting work recently carried out, however, revealed a surprisingly different employment of these large expanses. Be it as it may that the *easternmost area* (and next to the nymphaeum) - that could be reached from the Colonnaded Street through a monumental staircase - might well have been a square, i.e., a sort of a forum apt for housing the metropolis's daily encounters and business dealings; the *central one*, instead, probably accommodated a luxuriant garden, whose plants, bushes and flowers were watered thanks to the

inevitable canalisation network. Easy as it is to imagine what an effect this vision of paradise might have had on Petra's visitors, it is thornier to envision their surprise once they discovered that the *third esplanade* was taken up by a large swimming-pool, with sides shaped as step-like terraces to allow for a descent into the water, and a rectangular-base pavilion placed at the centre. We must note that said basin may well have had a ceremonial function, just like the "sacred Egyptian lakes", but that is difficult to demonstrate. Nevertheless, in their capital-city, the Nabataeans

56

clearly wanted to demonstrate to the world all their ability as hydraulic engineers, and their absolute mastery over the most precious resource: water.

A little further on, at the end of the Colonnaded Street, and once accessible by walking up a monumental staircase, rises the so called "**Large Temple**", one of Petra's most mysterious monuments. Archaeological excavation carried out since 1993, has recently permitted an amazing discovery regarding this enormous structure, erected at the middle of the I century b.C., once deemed a peripteral worship edifice. First, in front of it, was a vast square court, paved with unusual hexagonal slabs, and flanked on its sides by two majestic porticoes, each supported by three rows of columns. The capitals surmounting this columned jungle were a very original Nabataean interpretation of the Ionic style, with four elephant heads placed at the corners, whose rolled-up proboscises took the place of the classical Ionic coil. From the large court - the outcome of a remarkable rebuilding effort occurring between the end of the I century A.D. and the beginning of the next-, two staircases ascended to the main building, also modified in the same years. The plan of this structure was rectangular, with a pronaos

56 Above: the Nymphaeum, rising next to a century-old tree and marking the beginning of the Colonnaded Street.

56 Below: a glimpse of the Colonnaded Street, once flanked on both its sides by porticoes under which there probably were shops and public houses.

57 Above: one of the capitals that crowned the columns of the porticoes placed opposite the "Large Temple", decorated with striking elephantine protomes.

57 Below: an overall view of the "Large Temple", with the large colonnaded court.

supported by columns leading to a teathron, a real miniature theatre, with more than 300 seats, whose elegant *cavea* is still perfectly visible. Since we are not sure what kind of activity - religious or secular? - was carried out inside this building – unequalled in the Middle East-, we are just as uninformed as to its purpose. It probably was, however, the seat of either the local government, the city's administration, or of some sort of public congregation, on the model of the Greek *bouleuteria* (buildings where the council of the

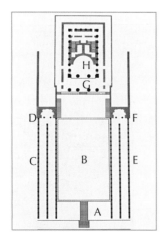

Plan of the "Large Temple"

A *propylaea*
B *large court*
  (or temenos?)
C *eastern colonnade*
D *eastern exedra*
E *western colonnade*
F *western exedra*
G *pronaos*
H *theatron*

58 Above: detail of the "Large Temple" front: the flight of stairs perhaps belonged to an earlier stage of the building's life (when it was really used as a temple).

58 Below: in this back view of the "Large Temple" you will notice how the intercolumniations were closed off at a later stage, to house the theatron.

town's representatives met). Waiting as we are for archaeological excavations to dispel the enigma, we still have to say that, in a few spots of the architectural complex, also some extremely rare remains of polychrome wall decoration have been unearthed, giving us a glimpse of the sumptuous looks of Petra's public buildings.

At the back of the "Large Temple", a few dozens of metres south-west, rises the isolated **Column of the Pharaoh**, the last standing testimony of what must have been either a temple, a palace or, anyhow, a big-sized monumental structure. Due to its aspect, the column is also known as Zibb Farawn (*zibb*

59 Above: clearly, the "Large Temple", erected perhaps to be a worship building, was eventually modified after the erection of the theatron, that took up the whole area of the cella. This ambience- it is thought-may have been the seat of government, or that of the town's council, but scholars even hypothesise that the structure was adapted as an odeon,

namely a kind of covered, small-sized theatre, to be found throughout the Roman empire.

59 Below, left: in the "Large Temple" traces of wall painting have been found.

59 Below, right: the pharaoh's column is what is left of a really big complex.

being a vulgar word for phallus). Nearby, on the hill known as ez Zantur, you will notice the diggings hitherto under way (and that cannot be visited), involving a large, two-storeyed house, erected during the I century A.D. on the foundation of an older construction. Other houses were explored in this city-sector and the (albeit modest) diggings are observable nearby.

On the opposite side of the Colonnaded Street, right in front of the "Large Temple", are the ruins of the **Temple of the Winged Lions**, so named due to a few unearthed capitals, decorated with the figures of these mythological animals. The excavation of this complex, beginning in 1974, permitted to understand that the worship building was preceded by a big bridge crossing the course of the Wadi Mousa - so that a first terrace could be reached-, surrounded by a colonnaded portico; from here, one ascended to a second court placed in front of the temple itself. This consisted in a large portico supported by mighty, still discernable under-structures which, through a portal, led to a square *cella*, paved with local marble and whose walls were emphasised by pilaster strips embedding deep niches. Five free columns on each side, in axis with the pilaster strips, were aligned on the eastern and western sides; at the centre, but shifted towards the northern wall, there was a high square platform (the *motab*), surrounded by 12 columns and accessible through two little stairways placed at the front, between the external intercolumniations. This platform performed as an altar, whereupon the

60 The Temple of the Winged Lions is typical of the first Nabatean monumental building, with its very close coloumns because of the difficulty in covering larger spaces. This was due to the inexperience of local architects as well as to a lack of long enough wooden beams. The problem was resolved later on by using stone trabeations

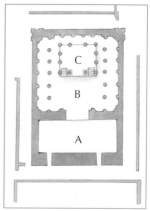

Plan of the Temple of the Winged Lions

A Pronaos
B Cell
C Motab

simulacrum of the goddess Al Uzza – to whom the temple is likely to have been consecrated - was worshipped; inside the *motab*, a little ambience was dug, similar to a crypt but accessible from the back, where sacred vestments were, perhaps, kept. Columns and walls were covered with marble slabs in the lower part, with painted stucco in the upper.

61 The monumental Door of Temeno is quite like a Roman Arc of Triumph. In fact, by the style of the low-reliefs that adorn the eastern side, but most of all the western side,

today one tends to date it to the Severian era - 193-211DC -. What is certain is that the monument was constructed on the site of an older, similar structure.

In the temple a famous stele was found exhibiting deeply stylised human features, identified as those of goddess Al Uzza, assimilated with Isis: nowadays it is to be seen in the New Museum (p. 66). The building is likely to date from the I century b.C., but it was rehashed several times and damaged by earthquakes in 113 (or 114) and 363.

Next to the temple, to the west, you will notice that a built up area, two shops for metal and marble processing, besides the atelier of a painter or decorator, are being excavated. On the opposite side, the ruins of an enormous building have still to be investigated: the same was also once faced by a big bridge, which, short as we are of irrefutable data, has received a suggestive but unreliable name, Royal Palace. A little further on, along the banks of the Wadi Mousa, stands out the rubble of a large tower, perhaps of the Byzantine age.

To the west, the Colonnaded Street terminates with the remains of a monumental arc with three barrel-vaults, today known as the **Door of Temenos**. Partly put back together thanks to a patient anastylosis, the structure was made precious with rich sculptured decorations, where busts of divinities alternated with smart rosettes. Though the aspect of the monument has for a long time made scholars think of it as a truly Roman triumphal arch erected to honour emperor Trajan, it actually was a real doorway that stopped access to the contiguous, under-the-sky sacred area (the *temenos*, in fact); this is also demonstrated by the fact that the structure, which was slightly oblique compared with the Colonnaded Street, is in axis, instead, with the holy precinct. The current structure, dating from Roman times (which explains its special shape), was built upon a similar, older building. We must observe that the part facing the road was - from the architectural viewpoint - more articulated, with four free columns (absent on the opposite side) animating its front; a part of the sculptural decoration (a head of Hermes, a bust of Dushara and one of Ares, a winged Tyche), is visible at the New Museum. In the stone threshold placed in the central barrel-vault, you can still see the two holes where the hinges of the heavy wooden doors turned, separating the silence of the *temenos* from chaotic daily life. On the sides of the door rose two tower-like structures, still to be interpreted; the one on the left served as a vestibule for a colonnaded

to date the sacred area (which had risen in a zone previously taken up by dwellings) back to the second half of the I century b.C., but even the colossal monument for which the *temenos* was built, namely the **Qasr el Bint**. The impressive building is the only one among those erected at Petra from their foundations to have been handed down to us relatively well kept, so much so that its ruins attain a height exceeding 20 m. Once the big

room, which in turn led to three hypogeous ambiences, covered with cupolas (cannot be visited); once they were believed to pertain to a thermal complex, but currently they are considered a worship centre or, anyhow, a bigger edifice, perhaps linked to the Large Temple. On the southern side (meaning to the left arriving from the Colonnaded Street), the0 **Temenos** still appears to be delimitated by an approx. 75 m long wall, on which two continual rows of seats leant, perhaps prepared to welcome priests and the faithful during holy celebrations; the northern side must have been arranged similarly, but the floods of the Wadi Mousa erased all traces of Nabataean brickwork. Several structures that looked onto the sacred area, are now merely rubble. One of the latter, near the monumental door, must have been a small prostyle temple. On a block of sandstone, embedded in the southern wall of the *temenos* at a later date than that of the building of the precinct itself, a dedicatory inscription to king Aretas IV was discovered in 1964, and another similar one was found in 1990; besides the fact that the two lithic blocks possibly supported statues (this suggesting that other sculptures ornamented the precinct of the *temenos*), their presence has permitted not only temple was believed to have been built in Roman times, but now it is a renowned fact that it was inaugurated in the second half of the I century b.C., perhaps in the reign of Obodas III (30-8 b.C.). Actually, the proportions and the configuration of the building are to be considered typically Nabataean: a square plan, north-south orientation, built with well squared sandstone blocks, bound together with mortar, its side measured 23 m, and

62 View of the temenos, the sacred area on which both the Qasr el Bint and also some minor sanctuaries, still to be excavated, stood. On the South side one notices a row of seats on which the audience sat during religious ceremonies.

62-63 The imposing mole of the Qasr el Bint, faced by the ruins of the great altar on which the priests used to officiate the public services. On the left, close up, one can see the exedra that closed the precinct of the sacred area to the West.

stood on a high podium faced by a staircase covered with marble. Heightwise, it must have attained about 29 m. The façade was of the *in antis* type, with four groove-less columns, plastered and topped by capitals, perhaps similar to those of el Khazneh. On the two lateral pillars was an unusual stucco decoration, displaying circles alternated with octagons.

The frieze ornamenting the entablature, that also ran along the other three sides of the building, consisted of triglyphs with extremely curious-looking metopes, shaped as round medallions with busts of divinities at their centre, alternated with couples of rosettes. Unfortunately, all the protomes were torn down by the iconoclasts (except for one, which is preserved in the Museum). The façade must have ended with a tympanum-like pediment, leaning on another parapet, and the building was probably covered with a flat roof, or with two slightly slanting slopes. As can be understood by observing the back wall, the whole temple was plastered with a thick layer of stucco, modelled and painted with architectural, illusionistic-flavoured side-scenes. Some evidence persuades us to suppose that, eventually, on the eastern and western sides of the temple, a low portico was added.

From the pronaos, through a high portal, which has lost its architrave - its upper disburdenment arc remaining miraculously in place-, you reach the *cella*, a big ambience whose plan is rectangular, illuminated by two large windows, opening high up in the short sides. It is easy to imagine that all the internal walls of the temple were plastered and painted. Three contiguous chambers look onto the *cella*: the central one, or **adyton**, probably housed the images of godly beings, for worship purposes. This ambience, whose walls were emphasised by

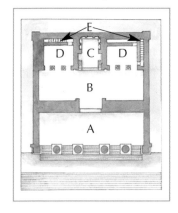

Plan of the Qasr el Bint

A Pronaos
B Cell
C Adyton
D Lateral Cells
E Stairs

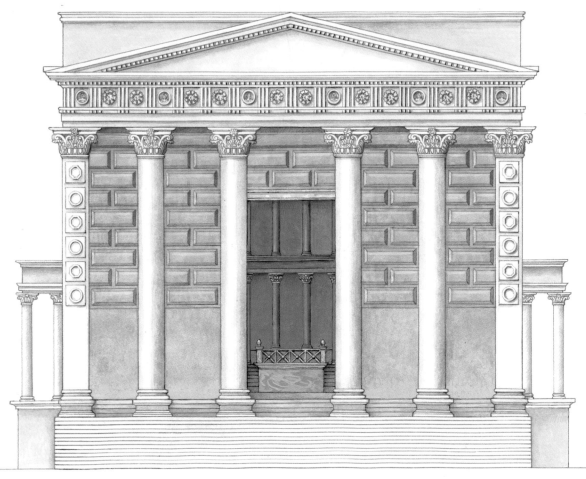

pilaster strips, was 1 1/2 m higher related to the *cella* floor, and you could reach it by going up two lateral stairways. The rooms at the sides, where perhaps symposia honouring deities took place, were arranged on two floors, and the mezzanines leant on couples of columns; access to the upper floors was ensured with two staircases built into the thick perimeter walls. It is also likely that these stairways, or at least one of them, led to the flat roof, or, anyhow, to a terrace where, perhaps, religious ceremonies were officiated, just as occurred in Egyptian temples (e.g., at Dendera). Now the temple, also due to its pre-eminent position and considerable sizes, is believed to have been consecrated to the two main Nabataean deities, Dushara and Al Uzza, though such a supposition has not been confirmed by any archaeological discovery so far. The full name identifying the monument is Qasr el Bint Farawn (namely, "Palace of the Pharaoh's daughter"), referring to the nth Bedouin legend, lacking whatever historic foundation.

In front of the Qasr el Bint, the *temenos* is partly taken up by the remains of a large rectangular altar, oriented along the east-west axis, about 13 m long and currently little less than 3, provided with a staircase; here sacrifices took place honouring the mightiest divinities of the Nabataean pantheon.

In the north-western corner of the *temenos*, behind the big altar, the ruins of a monumental Roman age building were recovered recently, furnished with an exedra flanked by columns and niches. Fragmentary inscriptions referring to 161-169 A.D.

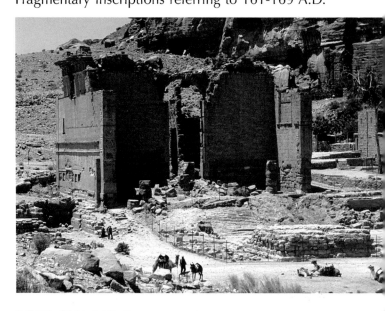

64 Hypothetical reconstruction of what the Qasr el Bin must have looked like. It is interesting to add here that in the walls juniper wood beams have been found, which were probably inserted for anti-sismic reasons. The same technique was used in the 'Great Temple'.

65 On the left: the external parameter of the Qasr el Bint was covered by modelled and painted stucco.

65 Above on the right: view of the temple and of the great altar opposite.

65 Below on the right: the inside of the building.

co-emperors Marcus Aurelius and Lucius Verus, and the finding nearby of their busts, make us believe that the building was dedicated to them. The exedra and Qasr el Bint were severely damaged by the 363 earthquake; during the crusaders' occupation, a part of the temple stone blocks were used to erect the castle topping the al Habis rock.

Nowadays, near Qasr el Bint, in an area known as Nazzal's Camp, you'll find toilets, a self-service refreshments facility, a souvenir shop and a restaurant, the latter adjacent to the **New Museum**,

built in the 1990s to house the relics unearthed during the various excavation campaigns carried out at Petra. In the modern and well lit rooms, you can admire sculptural fragments, Nabataean and Roman coins, jewels, daily life objects, mosaic floors patiently restored, besides a significant selection of extremely delicate Nabataean

66 Above left: one of the halls of the New Museum, whose collections include fragments of statues, pottery and objects of everyday use.

66 Below left: in the museum also this extraordinary capitel with elephantine traits is kept, which was discovered in the 'Great Temple'; the tusks must have been made of ivory or some other perishable material.

66 Right: a relief representing a sphinx, also in the museum.

67 Left: the magnificent and inspiring floors of the Byzantine church mix figurative Christian themes with others from the pagan Greek-Roman tradition.

67 Right: a foreshortened image of the Blue Chapel.

ceramics. In the first room also an extraordinary capital was recently placed, bearing elephantine protomes, the best-preserved amongst those uncovered amidst the "Big Temple" ruins. Now we only have to explain what lies under the showy white, stress resistant structure, well visible on the hill dominating the northern bank of the Wadi Mousa: this is a **Byzantine Church**, unearthed in the early 1990s and dating from the last decades of the V century. Since Petra was a bishop's seat, it is likely that here we had a cathedral. East-west oriented and displaying a basilica plan, its façade

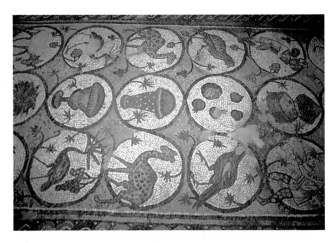

preceded by an atrium, the naves supported by columns ending with three apses; it must have been sumptuously decorated with wall-mosaics. Whilst the central nave floor is not well preserved, the fate of the lateral ones has been different, covered as they are by elaborate mosaics, too. The latter included theories of geometric cornices featuring personages, animals and objects, linked with Christian liturgy, and classical tradition as well. In a ambience next to the church, 140 manuscript rolls were unearthed, most of them legal documents of an influential local family's three generations

(contracts, registrations of landed estates, receipts of payments, etc.). Though damaged by a fire that destroyed the church (perhaps in the VII century), having turned out to be quite readable, they are still the subject of studies, casting light, as they do, onto Petra's Byzantine age social life.

North of the church, next to the city's enceinte and on the dorsal summit dominating the valleys of both Wadi Mousa and Wadi Turkmaniyya, recent archaeological diggings unearthed the foundations of a Nabataean edifice - now known as the Ridge Church - converted into a church during the second half of the IV century. In the area extending between the latter and the Byzantine Church, taken up in Nabataean times by residential quarters, another small building was discovered, also changed into a church, perhaps during the first years of the VI century. The structure has been given the name of **Sky-blue Chapel**, due to the unusual columns made of bluish Egyptian granite, coming from a more ancient Nabataean monument, and only recently lifted through anastylosis work, which also restored us with their Nabataean-type capitals. The little church building is believed to have been contiguous with the palace of Petra's bishop.

ITINERARY IV - EL DEIR**

Though the walk up to el Deir (or Monastery) is undeniably long, steep and quite exhausting, we must consider it practically mandatory since the destination is one of the most spectacular monuments at Petra and of all the ancient world. We advise you to start the walk in the afternoon, because the deep valley will be in the shade for long stretches then, the façade of el Deir faces west and so it appears in full light just in the second half of the day. As always, you had better take along at least a litre of water, though

at arrival you will find a comfortable Bedouin tent where you can drink and refresh yourselves. The path is easy to walk along, but you had better wear proper shoes for a march; whoever is less athletic can travel on a handy donkey to complete the ascent; otherwise you'll take about 40 minutes on foot. The overall itinerary requires no less than 3 hours.

The walk begins near the New Museum and is clearly indicated. First, the path heads north-west along the dry bed of the Wadi Kharareeb, which on both sides

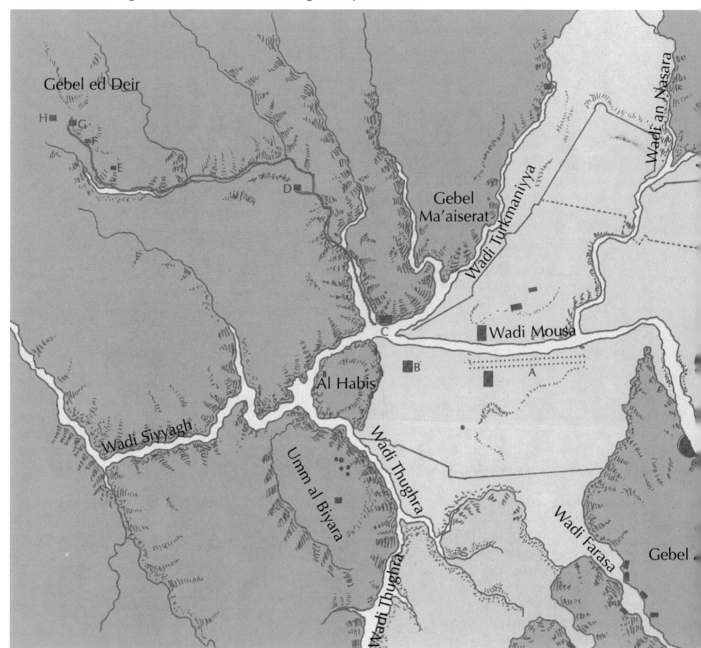

appears to be controlled by a myriad of rock-cut tombs built in the most different styles. Quite soon the ancient Nabataean road appears, carved out of rock for long stretches, now with a slight difference in level and embedded in sandstone (at one point, an ancient tremor provoked the fall of a boulder, which, while partly blocking the path, originated quite a fascinating "arc"), now changing into unending stairways, which all together amount to about 800 steps.

When you arrive at a fork (partly hidden to one's sight by the view of the oleanders), a signpost indicates the presence of the **Triclinium of the Lions,** which can be reached by walking along a short and uneasy side-road on the left. The rocky structure, often erroneously described as a tomb, is quite interesting

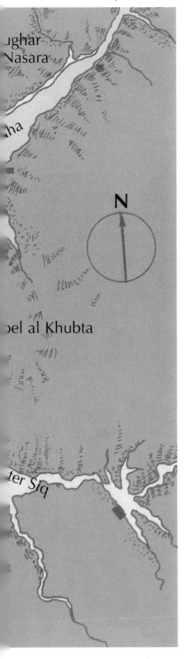

A Colonnaded Avenue
B Qasr el Bint
C Museum
D Triclinium of the Lions
E Qattar ed Deir
F Christian Hermitage
G Deir -'The Monastery'-
H Monument 468

69 Left: the Deir is probably the grandest work of the Nabatean architects; by looking at the person in the picture one can estimate its huge size.

69 Above right: detail of the superb facade of the Deir.

69 Below right: the Triclinium of the Lions owes its name to the two reliefs carved at the sides of the entrance.

because it is one of the few tricliniar chambers handed down to us nearly intact; moreover, the façade, carved into the front wall of the narrow, deep valley - next to a couloir (or *steep gully on the mountain side*)-, is quite nice. Of the pediment type, it is framed between two pilaster strips with quarters of columns leaning on it, and capitals decorated with racemes; the entablature, presenting a Doric frieze where triglyphs alternate with paterae, is concluded at its two extremities by two unusual Medusa heads, which luckily survived the iconoclasts' fury and are still well decipherable. The pediment, whose tympanum is made precious by vegetable motifs, bears on the summit an acroterium shaped as an urn. The portal, before which there is a staircase carved in sandstone, is flanked by two reliefs featuring lions (animals that were sacred to goddess Al-Uzza) that gave the name to the monument. The door opening was surmounted by an oculus, but earthquakes and erosion brought forth a strange profile resembling a "keyhole".

While returning by the side of the main path, you keep on following the Wadi ed Deir along the

70 Left: the Triclinium of the Lions is datable to King Aretha IV's reign, but some retain it to be subsequent to the Roman conquest -106 a. D.

70 Above right: next to the Triclinium of the Lions there is a great betyle

consecrated to Dushara and two tombs, in close relation to the tricliniar chamber.

70 Below on the right: the Christian Hermitage also includes a room that looks onto the void.

Nabataean stairways in an increasingly exciting scenario; the most curious tourists (better if accompanied by a boy of the place), by following a deviation to the right, shall be able to get as far as the enormous cistern known as Qattar ed Deir, one of the few that are still fed by a perennial spring, near which numerous betyles, inscriptions and graffiti can be seen. There where the Nabataean road enters into an impressive gorge, forming an airy belvedere of candid sandstone allowing you to see the Wadi Siyyagh in the distance, it is worthwhile concentrating your attention onto the rocky promontory rising to the left. That is where a few natural cavities are to be seen at a few metres of altitude, connected the one with the other and jutting out onto the void: though their original function is unknown, it is certain that in Byzantine times these rooms were adapted as a **Christian hermitage**: this is indicated by a few crosses and other Christological symbols engraved in one of the chambers. Outside, not easily distinguishable, you will notice three crosses carved out of the rock which date from the period of the crusades. We warn you not to go up, also due to the frequent presence of scorpions.

A quite airy, short stretch and a few more flights of steps lead you at last to the mountainous col opening out at the foot of the Gebel ed Deir, in whose sides the amazing façade of **El Deir (or Monastery)** is carved. The presence of the mighty monument is announced by the sight of the colossal urn topping its *tholos* appearing unexpected, from behind a side-scene of rocks. The façade of the rocky edifice, however, is placed many metres back related to the

71 Left: on the knoll of light sandstone, placed just in front of the Christian Hermitage, there is an incredible staircase dug out of the rock; curiously, it looks like it does not lead anywhere, but it is an example of the extraordinary ability of the Nabatean stone-cutters.

71 Right: along the hill leading to the Deir one can admire a few strange natural formations and splendid views. Shortly before reaching the Deir, a short short-cut on the right leads to the Quattar ed Deir, an enormous Nabatean cistern, still fed by a perennial source.

side of the mountain, so that its view appears suddenly, leaving you speechless for the dimension and purity of the architecture. The sizes of this authentic masterpiece are extraordinary – m. 50 (width) by 45 (height) – but was is really amazing is the absolute perfection of its outline, which may be appreciated in all its magnificence even thanks to the nearly flawless state of the monument. The contrast amongst the crazily eroded rocks surrounding the building and its austere majesty increases the sense of marvel and respect; seen from the side, the building looks as if it were freeing itself from the mass of brute rock as per a miracle, transforming the incoherent sandstone forms into an unheard-of geometric theorem.

The façade is highlighted on two floors, marked by pilaster strips topped by the usual Nabataean capitals; in the lateral intercolumniations, two niches topped by curved tympanums are hollowed out. The 8 m high portal, which is also embedded between two pilaster strips, was originally preceded by a staircase. Another split entablature bears the second floor, engraved in very high relief and comprising two door-shaped avant-corpses and two semi-pediments framing the central *tholos*, in turn covered by a conical roof concluded by an enormous Nabataean capital supporting a great urn (the ensemble alone is 9 m high!). The three great rectangular niches opening in the *tholos* and in the semi-pediments must originally have housed (as the two underlying ones) some full-bodied statues or – based on the type of the Tomb of the Roman Soldier (p. 79) – some polychrome high reliefs. The architectural elements of the second floor are interlinked by a very elegant, continual Doric frieze, where the usual triglyphs alternate with metopes consisting in scarcely outlined discs. We must remark that the very successful contrast between the concave line of the entablature above the portal and the convex line of the *tholos* indicate the influence of Hellenistic architecture, and also represent an amazing anticipation of baroque architecture. Generally speaking, the rhythmical alternation of straight and curved lines, the chiaroscuro games amongst masses and voids, the use of typically Nabataean elements such as the "horned" capitals and the circular metopes, indicate not only the perfect blend of heterogeneous stylistic elements, mostly from the Hellenised world, but also the peculiar singularity of Nabataean architecture.

In the past, el Deir was believed to be king (70-106 A.D.) Rabbel II's tomb and the last big monument to have been erected at Petra; several considerations,

72 The Deir still remains an enigmatic monument: even if we can be relatively sure it was not a tomb, the period of its construction is still uncertain. Some authors consider it to be the last great Nabatean monument, in which the relative absence of decoration -typical of the Khazneh- would be nothing but a local reaction to the Greek style, which was believed to have become too heavy. The only certain fact is that it was certainly not a monastery, as its present name suggests; the muddle was created by the fact that the monument was used as a church for a certain time during the Byzantine period, as is certified by the presence of a few

however, now underlie the proposal for radically different dates and functions. First of all, since the internal chamber - (a die whose diameter is 11 m, lacking ornaments except for a large arcosolium niche carved into the wall at the end) - shows no traces of loculi, it seems evident that it is not a sepulchre. The presence of two long benches along the side walls would seem to demonstrate that this was a *biclinium* (wholly similar to a tricliniar hall), but the sort of altar inserted inside the arcosolium makes us suppose that here there was a sacred image. Moreover, the presence along the processional road of an inscription mentioning the "symposium of Obodas, the god", allows us to surmise that el Deir was a *heroon*, i.e. a temple-cenotaph commissioned to commemorate the figure of a deified monarch. This king should be Obodas I (96-87 b.C.), who died, and was perhaps buried, at Advat, a Nabataean town in the Negev (today in Israel), and the purpose of the hall might have been to house banquets, symposia and ceremonies honouring him. Additionally, the façade of the temple faces just west, there where the ancient caravan centre rises. To end with, considering the sobriety of the monument (lacking whatever decorative element of a figurative type), the uninhibited employment of peculiarly Nabataean

elements, the fact that it is named after king Obodas I, as well as the recent dating of el Khazneh, we might conclude that the monument dates from the I century b.C. and that it must be considered, therefore, the prototype of great monumental Nabataean architecture, of which el Khazneh itself and the Corinthian Tomb should be thought of as the subsequent and most elaborate developments.

In connection to the worship of king Obodas I, perhaps also linked to that of the god Dushara, might be also the vast esplanade opposite the rock-cut edifice, which used to be surrounded on three sides by a colonnaded portico: its existence is indicated by the pilaster strips carved in the rock, still visible on the

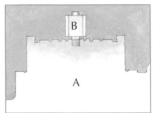

Plan of the Deir

A Courtyard
B Chamber or Biclinium

73 Left: with its nine metres of height, the cone-shaped covering of the tholos confirms the exceptional size of the Deir; just the doorway is about eight metres tall.

73 Right: viewed from the side, the huge figure of the Deir seams to detach itself from the living rock as if by magic.

73

front of the two rocky prominences to the right and the left of el Deir, as well as by the column drums buried in the sand, some of which are still visible. This court, where those who celebrated the sacred functions perhaps gathered, was crossed by the processional road, which went on further, after passing by a large rocky altar which can still be distinguished.

The aspect of the whole el Deir area – where other hypogea, canalisations, cisterns and niches can be noticed – once was likely to be quite different; probably a vast worship zone, besides being one of the entrances to Petra, given that you can get here from Al Barid, i.e., Little Petra (p. 104). These considerations could explain the existence of a great circular esplanade, whose diameter is 60 m, partly cut into the rock and placed between el Deir and the rocky buttress rising opposite, to the right; in such a vast space (which could be assimilated to a "high place of sacrifice"), a large crowd of faithful could indeed assemble. In the sharp, rocky projection we just mentioned, a wide, cubic, façade-less chamber opens up, today known as **Monument 468** in Brünnow's classification; this ambient was the *cella* of a very big edifice (perhaps one of Petra's biggest), preceded by a powerful masonry sub-structure that probably supported an enormous pronaos composed

at its front by 14 or 16 columns, whose bases can still be seen *in situ*. A monumental staircase, placed to the right, must have brought up to this edifice, razed to the ground by one of the terrible earthquakes that shook this region in the past. Inside the hall you can admire Petra's most elaborate and best preserved aedicule: it consists in a niche where the image of the god was placed, closed between pilaster strips, surmounted by a Doric entablature similar to the one of el Deir, and framed between two other semi-pillars supporting an entablature with a smooth frieze, but decorated with two busts at its extremities; the whole thing, whose taste is clearly Hellenistic, is topped by a pediment with three acroteria. Please notice that the ascent to such ambient is not easy and may result dangerous.

At the entrance to the second deep valley unfolding to the left of the el Deir façade, amongst cisterns, stairways and canalisations, we can still see, by the side of a hypogeum door, a very worn out relief featuring two Nabataean merchants, each one leading a dromedary by its reins: the group recalls the one discovered in the Siq.

To end with, the attentive eye shall notice that the whole north-western part of the mountainous col is full of rubble (stone blocks, column drums, remains of mighty stonework, etc.), suggesting that several

structures stood here whose function is unknown. These ruins – amongst which, perhaps, the propylaea that led to the sacred area – confirm again that this place must have been full of monuments in the antiquity.

The descent to Petra takes place along the same itinerary we followed for the climb; under no respect do we suggest to reach "Little Petra" from el Deir without the aid of a local guide.

74 Above: the aedicula (niche) inside Monument 468 is the best conserved in all of Petra.

74 Below: in the picture one can see the rocky relief in which the enormous rocky area of Monument 468 is dug as well as the mountain ridge facing it, littered with ruins and lithic blocks.

75 Above: from the top of the hills located to the North-West of the Deir, one has a spectacular view of the wadi Siyyagh below and on the more distant wadi Arabah.

75 Below: the relief, very eroded, shows two Nabatean merchants with their dromedaries.

ITINERARY V - THE GEBEL ATTUF ***

Though the ascent to the Gebel Attuf and to the "high place of sacrifice" to be found on the top of the mountain is quite exacting and tiring – even more than the one leading to el Deir –, in all cases it really deserves to be taken into consideration, for the interest of its rock-cut monuments, to be met with along the way, as well as for the spectacular panoramas to be enjoyed. The itinerary described here (lasting at least 3 h) can obviously be followed in the two directions, but you had better know some

of its features. The processional road starting from the outer Siq, shortly after Tomb 70 (p. 41) and before the Theatre, is signalled and can be easily found, but quite soon changes into a never ending succession of rock-carved stairways, as suggestive as they are steep. The narrow, deep valley along which they climb up is sun-beaten during the whole second half of the morning, thus making the march even more laborious, above all when there is no wind. The climb from the Wadi Farasa, instead, is

A El Khazneh
B Theatre
C Colonnaded Street
D Qasr el Bint
E Column of the
   Pharaoh
F Tomb of the Split
   Pediment
G Tomb of the
   Renaissance
H Tomb of the Roman
   Soldier
I Triclinium
J Tomb of the al Najr
K Garden Tomb
L Monument of the Lion
M Obelisks
N High Place for
   Sacrifices

much more gradual and, even if the path is under the sun for the whole afternoon, it is less tiring thanks to the frequent whiffs of wind; if you begin your walk during the hottest hours of the day, you'll be able to complete the excursion enjoying repeatedly the shade afforded by the numerous rocky ambiences placed along the way, and you'll reach the top of the Gebel Attuf in ideal conditions of light to fully appreciate the majestic view over the whole city of Petra and the surrounding mountains. The descent, at the end, shall take place in restoring shade and, once you get to the outer Siq, you won't be very far from the gate leading into the archaeological area. Should you want to follow this piece of advice then, the itinerary shall begin behind

76 Above: view of the wadi Farasa, dominated by the Gebel Attuf Rock: the path climbs up the ravine in the shade, on the right in the photograph.

76 Below: the Tomb of the Roman Soldier is the best known example of monument in the 'classic Roman style'.

77 Above: the Tomb of wadi al Najir, unfortunately, is a hardly visited monument.

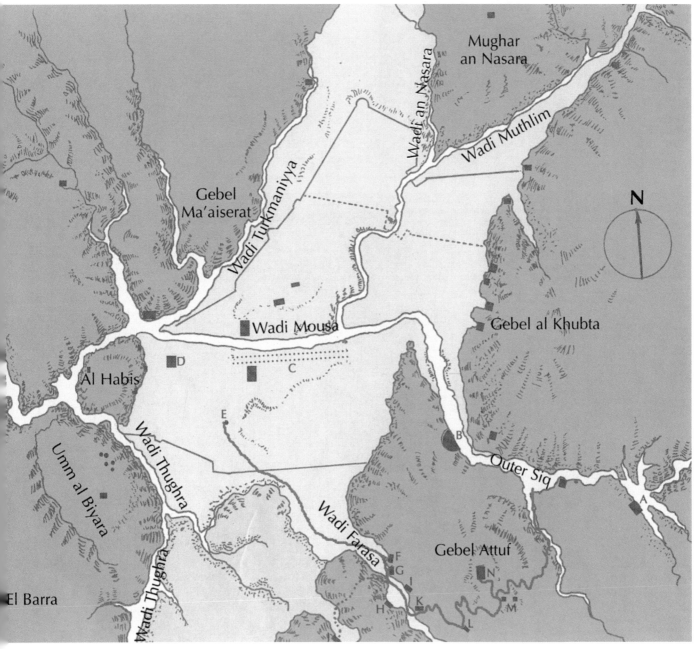

the Great Temple, near the isolated "Pharaoh's Column" (p. 59); the pathway, well visible, heads south-east and goes through the Wadi Farasa. The rocky walls to the left are 'pockmarked' with rocky façades placed on several levels, in a fashion which is not different from that of the outer Siq (especially one - eroded by the wind, and very photogenic-looks like a mask with its mouth wide open). Quite soon you'll be able to recognize the **Tomb of the Split Pediment**, surely one of Petra's most balanced structures from a stylistic viewpoint.

Carved in a rocky offshoot facing north, in a position

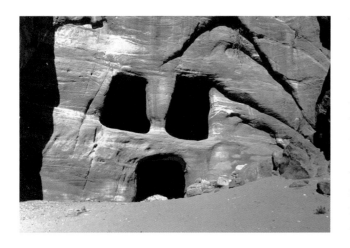

which is higher related to the track and opposite a wide courtyard cut into sandstone, it comes as a unique piece, where the contrast between formal Hellenistic schemes and the Nabataean taste for the superimposition of decorative elements seems to be well achieved. The façade is marked by four prominent pilaster strips with "horned" capitals, on which a simple entablature leans supporting a split pediment. The frame of the door, reached by a short stairway, was probably damaged by an earthquake, that, then, explaining its unusual aspect; inside you will notice four loculi, whilst a few other ones were never completed. The little ambience to the right of the tomb probably was a *triclinium*; on the terrace before the tomb two ample cisterns were carved, one of them square-shaped, the other octagonal.

Shortly after the tomb with the split pediment you meet with the elegant **Tomb of the Renaissance**, whose name is due to the magnificent proportions. The façade is embedded between the usual pilaster strips with a quarter of a column leaning on it, bearing an entablature with a smooth frieze and a tympanum, not built to be very high, and surmounted by three acroteria. The portal, whose shapes curiously recall Italian Renaissance architectural stylistic features, though framed

according to the classical Nabataean canons, is however inserted within a second framing, formed with the usual semi-pillars with half a Nabataean capital on which an open pediment with a lowered arc leans, instead of the normal entablature, on whose extrados are three little urn-shaped acroteria. Given the formal resemblance with Sextus Florentinus's Tomb, this monument is likely to date from the first half of the II century A.D., too.

Shortly further on, there where the Wadi Farasa narrows and becomes steeper, you reach the awesome **Tomb of the Roman Soldier**, opposite an esplanade, partly rock-carved, and its great *triclinium*. The façade, set in the wall facing west, is the most celebrated and complete example of "classic Roman style" (together with the non-distant, but hardly visited, Tomb of al Najr, in the wadi bearing the same name), and recalls a tetrastyle temple front very much. On the sides, it is embedded between two pilaster strips with a quarter of a column leaning on it, whilst the portal is included within two pilaster strips; the very much eroded capitals seem to be of the usual Nabataean type, while the frieze-less entablature, supports a

78 Above: along the path one encounters this bizarre rocky structure, which the winds have eroded and made look like a mask.

78 Below: in the Tomb of the Broken Pediment, the lintel (architrave) of the door is very ruined, but it must have been of the usual simple entablature kind. The two narrow loopholes that open between the couples of semi-pillars are decisively of a later period and were probably opened in the crusader era, when the tomb was used as a small fortification or as a look out.

79 Also in the Tomb of the Renaissance, the two small loopholes that one notices at the sides of the entrance are once again the result of a subsequent intervention, probably datable to the crusader occupation of Petra.

low tympanum, perhaps originally decorated with three acroteria and in its own turn set within a rectangular parapet. The portal is topped by a pretty Doric frieze bearing a tympanum. The peculiarity of the tomb lies in the three niches carved high up in the intercolumniations, framed by pilaster strips and a smooth entablature, inside which just as many high relief statues can be detected very well. The central one, lacking its legs and head, portrays a man wearing a cuirass of the Roman type, whilst the ones standing at its sides - also, unfortunately, very worn out - seem to depict two males wearing a short military tunic; the few surviving traces of stucco

prompt us to think that the figures were polychrome. The central personage is held to be a high-ranking Roman soldier (or, perhaps, even an imperial legate) and the other two his children; judging by the kind of dress and by the general features of the sepulchre, the tomb is believed to have been carved in the first decades of the II century A.D. The interior of the tomb consists of two square-layout funerary chambers; into the walls of the first one several arcosolium-like loculi were carved.

Extremely recent archaeological diggings (still under way in 2006) were carried out in the vast court unfolding in front of the tomb. These have proven

Plan of the Roman Soldier's Tomb

A Colonnaded Courtyard
B Funerary chamber

C Secondary Funerary Chamber
D Burial Niches
E Triclinium
F Service Rooms (?)

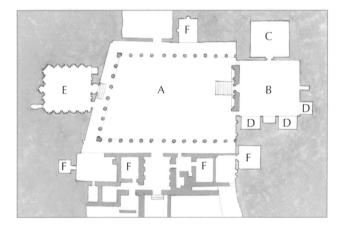

80 Above: the Roman Soldier's Tomb was originally faced by a colonnaded courtyard. Over the facade one can notice a deep rectangular room, which could be of a precedent tomb that may have been dug up to make room for the new sepulchre.

80 Below: judging by the sort of armour worn by the character in the high relief which one finds in the central intercolumniation, one can suppose that the tomb is of the first decades of the second century a. D.

that the area (secured by levelling off the bottom of the wadi and by regimenting the water course, fuelled during the rainy periods) was surrounded on the three sides by a portico supported by columns; moreover, the side of this portico facing the deep valley, supported by a retaining wall, surely included several other accessory ambiences, placed on two floors. The chamber just in front of the tomb was a large *triclinium*, unique in its kind at Petra because of its elaborate decoration. The multicoloured walls, in fact, are emphasised by a sequence of grooved pilaster strips, topped by capitals whose shape is very unusual, and

supporting an entablature whose cornice is continual; in the high part of the intercolumniations, rectangular niches open out, which were once surmounted by a stone frame embedded in a befitting groove (only a few have remained *in situ*). The bench running along three sides of the hall indicates the primitive function of the chamber. The excavations of the Roman Soldier's Tomb establish beyond any doubt that, in Nabataean funerary architecture tombs, their tricliniar halls and the porticoed courtyards formed a single indissoluble unit, and must have been the norm, not the exception.

81 Above:
he delicate flutes still visible on the trunks of the columns of the triclinium, make one think that the walls of the chamber were neither plastered nor painted - entablature and ceiling surely were, as one can infer from the well recognizable traces -; on the other hand, the magnificent polychromatism of the sandstone is a masterpiece in itself which it would not have made much sense to cover. One should notice that the capitals of the semi-columns look like a new fusion of the Ionic,

81 Below:
the Tomb of al Najir is unfortunately rarely visited, even if it is of considerable interest for the architectonic characteristics that render it similar to the Roman Soldier's Tomb. Also, the triclinium near it is peculiar in that a few burial niches are dug into it; finally, in an adjoining tomb, the internal walls present pilaster strips, capitals and friezes carved in relief -a practically unique fact-. The wadi al Najir is situated on the right of the ravine in which the Roman Soldier's Tomb is located and can be reached with a ten minute walk.

If you keep on going along the Wadi Farasa, which here is possible thanks to a steep stairway, you'll soon reach another rocky structure, known as the **Tomb of the Garden**, carved in a spectacular position inside a jut of the rock. The front appears as a simple but suggestive portico with two columns *in antis*, surmounted by the usual Nabataean capitals and by an entablature, whose frieze is smooth. The interior consists in a slightly trapezoidal, bare hall leading into a second, smaller room, whose layout is square. The monument's name is due to the fact that Nineteenth century visitors saw the small court placed before the structure full of rubble and earth on which luxuriant oleanders grew; in reality, since in the hypogeum there is no evidence of loculi, it is quite likely that this was a small temple, placed here perhaps to "protect" the nearby, enormous cistern (as much as 18 m long, that must have supplied all this sector of Petra), whose awesome retaining wall of the southern side can be seen to the right of the structure. An extremely steep stairway climbs to the mouth of the cistern, but it is very dangerous, and it is better to go on along the path, which here begins to ascend along the precipitous slopes of the Gebel Attuf, often changing into steep stairways. Along the itinerary you also pass through a narrow fissure dug into the rock, which once was ostensibly furnished with a portal: this demonstrates the fact that Nabataean roads were easily garrisoned, and were part of the complex defensive system protecting Petra. From the path, at a certain point you enjoy quite a panoramic view over the underlying Tomb of the Roman Soldier and the contiguous Tomb of the Garden; you will also see the large cistern very well,

opposite which is a curious rectangular room, once covered by an unusual barrel vault (by now collapsed) and in whose walls a theory of big rectangular niches open out. Perhaps, the mysterious ambience was a tricliniar hall, but this hypothesis seems quite doubtful. Along the path you also bump into the **Monument of the Lion**, which in reality was a monumental fountain. The large rock-cut animal is acephalous; the head, perhaps made of stone, or of metal, must have had its jaws wide open and the water, flowing from an upper cistern, gushed out from it. In the rock, you can still see very well the groove where the embedded piping was, in which the precious liquid flowed.

Not much far ahead, on the side of a buttress jutting over the abyss, a large rectangular betyle stands out, inserted in a double frame; above the niche you will notice a circular medallion inside which an unfortunately very worn-out bust is sculptured, which probably depicted god Dushara (according to other authors, goddess Al-Uzza). This is one of the rare figurative depictions of a Nabataean god.

The processional road– at times very airy – now decidedly climbs towards the top of the Gebel Attuf; before reaching destination, on the rocky walls the

82 Above: the area in front of the great cistern of the Tomb of the Garden.

82 Below: the so-called Tomb of the Garden was in reality a temple, maybe dug during the reign of King Aretha IV in the second half of the first century a. D.; recent excavations have uncovered a cistern located just in front of the hypogeum.
83 Above: the Roman

Soldier's Tomb, seen from the path that mounts to Gebel Attuf.

83 Below left: along the path one notices this betyle surmounted by a rare iconographic representation of a Nabataean god.

83 Below right: the Monument of the Lion is two metres and a half high and four metres and a half wide.

most attentive eyes will notice several votive inscriptions engraved in the sinuous Nabataean alphabet. Suddenly, you arrive at a mountainous col, kept vigil over by the amazing rock-cut **obelisks**. Actually, the summit of the Gebel Attuf (1,041 m) is divided into two: the part facing north is taken up by the "high place of sacrifice" (or Gebel Madhbah), whilst the southern one is indeed famous because of its two approx. 7 m high obelisks. Standing at about 30 m the one from the other, the monoliths rise isolated on an esplanade which was prepared by excavating the top of the mountain: it is a common opinion that they depicted the deities Dushara and Al-Uzza, but it is also just as likely that they had some astronomic function, given that they are aligned along the east-west axis.

The access to the **"high place of sacrifice"** is guarded by an isolated, ruined tower, which was a section of the fort erected on the location of a Nabataean quarry; according to some scholars, it was a crusaders' building, but it is likely that the structure, at least as far as its foundations are concerned, belongs to the Byzantine (or perhaps even Nabataean) age. The path passes right through the ruins, then turns left, till it reaches the summit of the massif. Here, preceded by a large cistern carved

in sandstone, you will find Petra's best preserved open-air shrine; at first, it won't seem so spectacular, but you had better remember that - in order to make this north-south oriented, rectangular court, about m 14 long and 6.5 wide, materialise - Nabataeans had to perfectly level off the top of the mountain! The centre of the area, delimited by a low step which perhaps served as a seat for whoever participated in the rites, is provided with a rectangular platform (the holy table) about 15 cm high, on which bloodless offers to the gods (spikes of wheat, food and beverages) must have been placed. On the western

84 Above: one of the Nabataean inscriptions visible on the path.

84 Below left: to obtain two obelisks, the Nabataeans had to excavate at least 3200 square metres of stone.

84 Below right: the Royal Tombs, seen from the peek of the Gebel Attuf.

side of the court, in front of the sacred table, a monolithic altar was carved, which is just a bit less than 1 m high, and preceded by three steps.

Since on its surface there is a square hole, it is becoming to think that here the betyle representing the god was plunged. To the left of the altar you will notice a rectangular cistern and a large circular basin, which can be reached along four steps and provided with a little groove for the outflow of liquids; it is believed to be a basin for holy water, where the blood of the victims (lambs, goats), immolated to the gods, was collected, or a pool used for the ablutions of priests.

If you go shortly beyond the sacred area, towards the northern edge of the Gebel Attuf, you will enjoy the most spectacular view over Petra's hollow and the Royal Tombs: such a panorama repays you of all your exertion.

To descend the valley you must retrace your steps, till you reach the foot of the watchtower and you're in view of the two monoliths (near which there is a refreshment-facility): from here, the track descends quite precipitously, right-bound, into a narrow, deep valley (notice the fronts of the ancient Nabataean quarries), which quite soon changes into an amazing series of stairways, in some spots quite eroded. Indeed, this is Petra's most spectacular processional way (besides being the one best preserved); the surrounding environment, the colour of the rocks, the aerial views onto the underlying outer Siq – together with the thought of the immense work that was required to build the road – make the descent from the Gebel Attuf one of the most vivid emotions granted by Petra.

85 Above left: the great round basin placed on the left of the altar.

85 Above right: the monolithic altar, with the hole in which the betyle representing the deity was fixed.

85 Below: 'The High Place for Sacrifices', with the sacred table in the centre.

Plan of the 'High Place for Sacrifices'

A Sacred Table
B Altar
C Purifying (lustral) basin

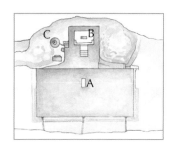

THE OTHER ITINERARIES

The itineraries hereafter proposed are recommended to those who wish to strengthen their knowledge of Petra and are prepared to endure a little additional strain. Since (apart from two exceptions) they usually cross less-trodden areas, be sure to have good footwear, an adequate supply of water and to be even more careful not to venture away from the paths.

86-87 A group of tombs along the wadi Ma'aiserat; all the area comprised between this valley and that of the wadi Turkmaniyya – in other words the slopes of the Gebel Ma'aiserat – is very rich in rocky structures: tombs in all styles, canalizations, enormous cisterns and even a 'High Place For Sacrifices'. To explore the area it is preferable to make use of a local guide.

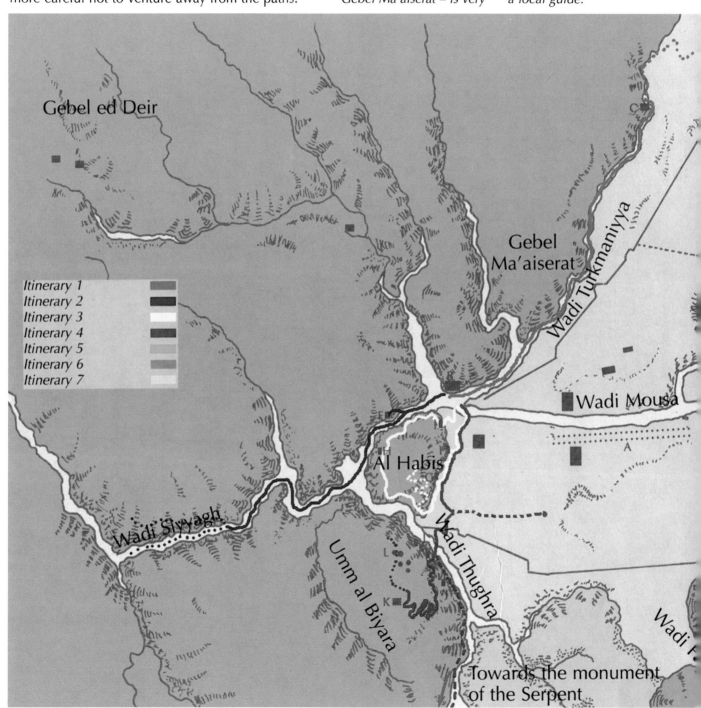

Gebel ed Deir

Gebel Ma'aiserat

Wadi Turkmaniyya

Itinerary 1
Itinerary 2
Itinerary 3
Itinerary 4
Itinerary 5
Itinerary 6
Itinerary 7

Wadi Mousa

Al Habis

Wadi Siyyagh

Wadi Thughra

Umm al Biyara

Towards the monument of the Serpent

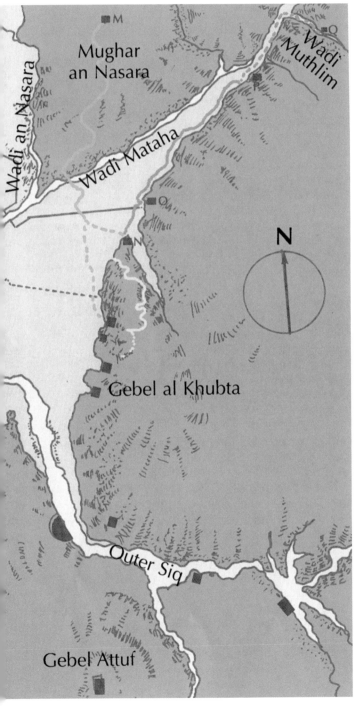

A Colonnaded Street
B New Museum
C Turkmaniyya Tomb
D Conway Tower
E Painted Room
F Unfinished Tomb
G Columbarium
H Convent
I Old Museum
J Southern Necropolis
K Edomite settlement
   on the 'Umm al
   Biyara
L Cisterns on the 'Umm
   al Biyara
M Tomb of the Suit of
   Armour
N Sextius Florentinus's
   Tomb
O Carmine Façade
P House of Dorotheos
Q Rock Shrine
   in the wadi Muthlim

89 Above, left: a glimpse
of Mughar an Nasara, an
area where there are
rather a lot of rock tombs.

89 Above, right: a
Nabataean graffito and
rock paintings – perhaps
Edomite – along the wadi
Siyyagh.

89 Below: two arc tombs
in the Southern
Necropolis, along the
wadi Thughra.

1- THE WADI TURKMANIYYA */**

This itinerary begins behind the New Museum, following the dirt road that goes along Wadi Turkmaniyya: consequently it is practicable without any difficulty. What immediately strikes the eye is the great number of oleander plants, which leads one to believe that in this area there is some abundance of water; as a matter of fact - furnished both by the usual canalisation system and by the wadi, whose river bed is copiously filled with water during the seasonal rains - here vast cultivations existed already in the days of the Nabataeans. The agricultural vocation of the area is still renewed, and along the road you can observe numerous orchards, the alternation of olive groves, -that the Bedouins manage to irrigate mostly by using the ancient hydraulic systems, connected to a modern aqueduct. On the right, in an elevated and quite suggestive position, a tomb stands out whose façade was carved in a tower of squared rock, last dregs of a Nabataean stone quarry. Other quarries can be seen along the entire valley. Even the unscientific calculation of the material extracted only in this area leads one to

believe that numerous buildings of big dimensions must have stood in Petra's hollow, more than we can ever imagine. Suddenly, once you have passed a slight curve on the left, you come upon the unmistakeable façade of the **Turkmaniyya Tomb**, easily recognizable because it has no lower half (probably eroded during the centuries by the disastrous floods of the wadi, or maybe intentionally demolished when the grave was used for other purposes). It is a grave with a double cornice, the front closed between two half pillars

with a quarter of a column leaning on it, and emphasized by two semi-columns that framed the entrance. The lower attic floor is measured by four short pilasters, in line with the ones below and, as these, crowned by the customary Nabataean capitals; two high, step-shaped merlons rise on the upper attic storey. The reason why the tomb is so important lies in the inscription carved into the central intercolumniation, below the rectangular niche, whose function remains unknown. Even though it does not mention the owner's name, it lists all the elements of the grave scrupulously,

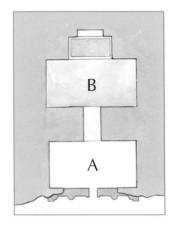

Plan of the Turkmaniyya Tomb: the darkest part corresponds to the section of the façade which was destroyed.
A. Vestibule
B. Funerary chamber

including the vestibule and the funerary room with their related loculi, the porticoed courtyard in front of the tomb, the *triclinium* (that is not far), the cisterns and the containment walls. All this property is then put under the custody of god Dushara with the comment that no one else can be buried in the tomb except for those entitled (namely, the children and relatives of the deceased). This epigraph, the longest ever discovered at Petra, was of fundamental importance for the study of the ancient idiom, but also for realising that, besides tombs proper, Nabataean burials included numerous additional structures, mostly destroyed by earthquakes and floods. Moreover, as the inscription was engraved on the façade itself- and not on a relief panel - it is evident that the front of this tomb was never coated with plaster. This contributes to the theory formulated by some whereby, originally, most of Petra's rock tombs were plastered and painted.
From here the slope of the road increases towards one of the secondary entrances to the archaeological area, and therefore it is advisable to return towards the Museum. The more curious tourists, nevertheless, can continue for another 100 m beyond the cluster of trees on the right of the track, then quit the dirt road and, with due

90 Left: the Turkmaniyya Tomb and the triclinium next to it.

90 Right above: one of the tombs situated along the wadi Turkmaniyya.

90 Right below: the Turkmaniyya Tomb was dated to the period in which Malichos II - 40 to

70 a. D.- reigned. It is not known who the legendary Turkmeno was, who gave his name to the burial.

91 Above: the inscription on the Turkmaniyya Tomb; theNabatean language was close to Aramaic.

91 Below: view of the valley of the wadi Mataha.

precaution, go up again along the side of the deep valley. Once you have reached the ridge, you shall be able to admire the sight offered by the multicolour sandstone banks, perforated by numerous ditch tombs, as well as by burials of the Assyrian and arched types. Turning to look towards Petra's ancient built-up area, on a rocky promontory which is not far away, you will note the ruins of a massive circular wall: this is the so-called **Conway Tower**, a bastion erected at the northernmost point of the urban enceinte. Since it surrounds an emergence, it is believed that it could be a sacred place reachable by a processional road, rather than a defensive apparatus. The hypothesis, however, must still be confirmed. For the return trip, we advise you to use the dirt road.

2- THE WADI SIYYAGH **

Also this– more demanding – itinerary begins close to the New Museum, from the modern reinforced cement bridge climbing over the dry riverbed of the Wadi Mousa. First of all, you must go down to the river bed of the torrent, partly transformed into a track that off-road vehicles can cross. Then head for the opening of the gorge

included between the rock of El Habis and the steep slopes of the Gebel ed Deir, there where the valley changes name to Wadi Siyyagh. About 100 m further on, to the right, you will see a sign where a brief but steep path begins, among clusters of aloes and oleanders. Quite soon, this changes into a short but rather exposed staircase, ending on the threshold of the so-called **Painted Room**, a part of a home where a very rare example of Nabataean wall-painting is preserved. Although the ambience – discovered only in 1979 – is closed with a barred door (the keys are in the museum, but it is difficult to get them), you can easily observe the plastered, vividly painted walls, with fake doors, panels and frames painted in red, yellow, orange and blue. The ceiling displays an unbelievable halo-like painting, whose fulcrum is a plaster rose, strikingly similar to those used in European homes until the middle of the last century. A similar, but better preserved rose, can be observed on the ceiling of an adjacent room, now lacking a wall.

From this privileged point of observation, you can see how the rock walls on both sides of the wadi teem with dozens of rocky ambiences, connected by dizzy ramps of stairs or by paths jutting out into the void: this was one of Petra's residential suburbs and evidently the Nabataeans did not suffer from giddiness. Everywhere the grooves of the aqueducts and the dark holes of the cisterns are to be seen. Moreover, one senses that many Nabataean rock houses had walls, exposed to the valley, constructed in masonry (where one or more windows opened), even if this structural element has been preserved only in a few cases. On returning to the river bed of the wadi, the more resistant and curious walkers shall be able to go on further, into a surreal world made of many-coloured rocks and blooming oleanders. The walls of the Wadi Siyyagh appear notched by the clean cuts of numerous Nabataean quarries, from where the necessary material was taken to build Petra's monuments; one in particular catches the eye for its boldness.

Where the gorge becomes narrower, the sudden vegetation growth reveals the presence of a perennial spring, partly canalized for irrigation purposes: here, today like in the past, the descendants of the Nabataeans cultivate olive and fruit trees. The place was especially sacred to the ancient deities, and this is confirmed by the numerous inscriptions covering the rock walls, together with "betyles" and other rock engravings

92 Left: the Conway Tower – at the centre, in the foreground – it owes its name to Agnes Conway, an English archeologist who worked in Petra in the twenties.

92 Right: the sides of the wadi Siyyagh are tunneled by dozens of rocky dwelling-places.

93 Left: an ancient quarry in the wadi Siyyagh: an obelisk is carved into it.

93 Right above, and centre: a detail of the frescoes with an architectural subject – in this case two, false doors – which decorate the so-called 'Painted Room' and the surprising ceiling with a sunburst decoration in the same area.

93 Below: this circular vault-centre in stucco is visible in a small room adjoining the 'Painted Room'.

of a sacred nature. Further on, spring-water gives origin to a series of small natural basins and even to a waterfall, but to go on further can be dangerous and, for the visit to the area, a local guide is highly recommended.

94 Left above: one of the inscriptions carved near the perennial source that runs into the wadi Siyyagh mentions the goddess Atargatis.

94 Left in the centre: graffiti on the sides of the wadi Siyyagh.

94 Left below: the source in the wadi Siyyagh feeds thick vegetation.

94-95 View of the low part of Petra: behind the al Qasr el Bint, the Rock of Al Habis can be seen, overshadowed in its turn by the towering mass of the Umm al Biyara.

95 Left: the imposing front of the Un-finished Tomb.

95 Right: the mysterious Columbarium, with its myriad of niches.

3 - EL HABIS */**

El Habis is an impressive rock dominating Petra's old built-up area, and towering on the Qasr el Bint and the New Museum: its perimeter at the base measures a little over 1 1/2 km. According to some, this was Petra's "citadel", i.e. an easily reachable and defensible place, in case of need; according to other authors, instead, it is the "acropolis", i.e., the nth sacred site. Curiously, its current Arab name means "The Prison". What is certain is that, at one time, most of the built-up area lay at El Habis' 's foot, with most of the main urban buildings, and that its slopes hosted a certain number of rock homes, in some of which slight traces of stuccoes and wall paintings remain.

The proposed itinerary is not particularly demanding, and it can be completed in a few hours, or little more; only the climb to the top of El Habis requires moderate physical exertion and a certain degree of attention, due to the exposure of the path. Since the point of departure and the one

of arrival are the same, choose the direction to take subject to the position of the sun, so that you remain in the shade for as long as possible during the journey. Nevertheless, the one suggested permits you to face the more exacting part first, leaving you after to enjoy a pleasant walk.

From the area known as Nazzal's Camp - where there is the restaurant -, a series of stairways climb

on the right of the Qasr el Bint, next to a fenced area, and heads towards the impending rock wall, and eventually runs along it in a slight but steady climb. At once the **Unfinished Tomb** catches your eye with its impressive façade. Its only finished parts are the architraves and, below, four Nabataean capitals; the outer-most ones should have topped the lateral pillars, the inner ones two high columns. Had it been finished, the façade would have stood with a huge portico *in antis* – similar to the one seen in "Little Petra" (p. 104) or at the Garden Tomb (p. 82) -, the biggest of its kind in all Petra. The reason why works were interrupted is unknown, but one may surmise that the hypogeum was meant to be a temple, not a tomb. A little further on from the Unfinished Tomb, on the left, rises one of Petra's most mysterious ambiences. We are talking about the so-called **Columbarium,** whose function is wholly obscure. The walls of the façade (which re-enters compared with the rock wall) as well as those of the internal ambience, are covered with a great number of

square niches, set out along regular rows. Such an arranged grid is broken off on the outside by a few bigger, rectangular niches. The Latin term "*columbarium*" means a type of burial in whose walls hollows were dug where cinerary urns were deposited; in this case, however, the niches are too small, and not deep enough to be used for such a purpose. It may be that this was a rock sanctuary, where, in the bigger niches, images of the deities were placed, while in the smaller recesses the faithful deposited offerings, votive lamps or small sacred images of the gods. The singular monument would have therefore resembled modern sanctuaries, where big numbers of ex votos accumulate; the hypothesis has still to be verified, however.

Leaving behind the "*columbarium*", we continue to go along the rock wall, quite soon passing in front of a hypogeum, occasionally occupied by a Bedouin family, that looks after the inevitable flock of goats (you can ask them further information about the surroundings); a little farther you will see a steep stairway cut into the rock climbing towards some old rock homes, situated in a position which is airy as much as it is spectacular. Also in this zone the path leading to the mount top begins: the route has been recently repaired, with the construction of new ramps and containment walls (and even of

a sort of "drawbridge"). Nevertheless, it is utterly un-recommended to those who suffer from dizziness. As a matter of fact, on the peak of El-Habis there is not much to see, if not the ruins of a crusaders' fort (that might have been built on the foundations of a Nabataean fortification), the scarce remains of a settlement dating from the Iron Age, and some traces of Nabataean worship areas. The view that is enjoyed from this elevated position, however, fully deserves the physical strain caused by the climb.

Those who have no propensity for ascents can continue the walk, going always along the slopes of the relief, till they reach the dirt road. On the left it leads towards the Pharaoh's Column (p. 59), on the right it heads north-west, running along the mountain relief wall (altitude of the path being halfway up the mount) and dominating the precipice of the deep valley of the Wadi Thughra. Quite soon, on the right, you will see some graves dug in the rock; on the north-western spur of El-Habis a beautiful pediment façade stands out, pertaining to a *tricliniar* room, and surmounted by a deep groove where an aqueduct ran. At the foot of the *triclinium* and, just along the dirt road, you will find a cavetto grave, in whose front two small

windows were opened. Faced by a charming garden, this is the home of Mofleh Bdoul, an old Bedouin with a natural sense of hospitality, who will be glad to offer you a cup of tea and chat in one of the many dialects that he learnt without ever leaving Petra.

A little further down, by following some flights of steps, you can reach a mysterious rocky complex, known as the **Convent**. This stands as a square courtyard, dug 6 m into the sandstone banks and surrounded on three sides by the entrances to several hypogea. It is popular opinion that this was the dwelling of the priests put at the head of the cults in the not so far "place of sacrifice". But it is much more probable that they be tombs dug inside a disused quarry.

On a rocky spur not far away, outstretched to dominate the underlying Wadi Thughra (here it comes together with the Wadi Siyyagh), we find the already cited "high place of sacrifice", somewhat similar to the one visible on Gebel Attuf, but smaller in size (about 5 m by 3.5 m).

We now return on the roadway, which from Mofleh Bedoul's home onwards changes into a real processional road cut into the rock. For many metres, the route is very airy, but entirely safe, and

96 Above: an nth curiosity in the Columbarium is that the niches are not cubic, while their back-walls are inclined toward the exterior, from the bottom upwards: this makes them inappropriate for housing urns, small though they be.

96 Below: the pediment-like façade of the triclinium dug into the slopes of Al Habis.

97 Left above: view of the mysterious complex of burial niches known as the 'Convent'.

97 Left below: the extremely steep ladder cut in the rock that from the wadi Siyyagh leads to the 'Convent'.

97 Right above: any stranger is welcome to a mint tea and a chat in the cosy home of Mofleh Bdoul.

97 Right below: even if it is less spectacular than the one on Gebel Attuf, the 'High Place for Sacrifices' situated behind the 'Convent' repeats all its principal characteristics, including the monolithic altar and the bench running all around the precinct.

97

your glance may hesitate on the deep valley below, encumbered with oleanders. The road brusquely turns right, and again you are in sight of Petra's hollow, just near the **Old Museum**. This is hosted in a hypogeum dug halfway up the mountain, and formed by three adjoining ambiences, whose original function remains unknown. However, it might have been a temple or, anyhow, a resting spot for the sacred processions that headed towards the "high place of sacrifice". Just few pieces of relief are preserved here (the findings of greater value are to be seen in the New Museum, or in Amman), but the amazing polychromatism of the walls really deserves a brief visit. On the terrace in front of the entrance, and along the ramps of steps that go down towards Nazzal's Camp, you can admire some other bas-reliefs, ornaments and sculptural fragments attesting to what remarkable degree Petra's ancient inhabitants were influenced by the artistic canons of Hellenism.

4 - THE THUGHRA WADI AND UMM AL BIYARA****

The valley of Wadi Thughra, opening between El Habis and the massif of Umm El Biyara, to continue south-east bound, is partly occupied by the vast, and still unexplored, southern Necropolis, where, among other things, you can admire a huge tomb with a double-frame. Nevertheless, we highly advise not to enter this sector of the archaeological area without a local guide; the risk of getting lost or of being injured - as well as the dehydration hazard - are not to be underestimated. You must take into account that, at Petra (above all in this sector), unfortunately grave –at time fatal - accidents have already occurred due mainly to irresponsibility. For the more curious, we wish to add that, continuing for about 1 h along Wadi Thughra, we find some djinn blocks, the mysterious Monument of the Snake, and the adjoining Tower Tomb (unique in its kind). A few km further (about 2 h walking) lies the Silent El Sabrah, a suburb of Petra where you can also admire a small rock theatre. Moreover, from the Southern Tombs begins a dizzy processional

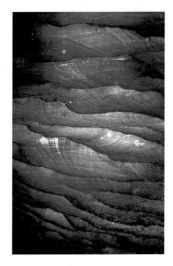

98 Above, left: the interior of the Old Museum, with the show-cases where some objects are still displayed.

98 Below, left: a detail of the many-coloured walls of the Old Museum.

98 Right above: in the Southern necropolis one notices the facade of a colossal tomb with a double: the path that climbs up from Umm al Biyara starts a few metres later on the left.

98 Right below: the steep stairs which lead to the peak of the Umm al Biyara have been restored, but the climb is still difficult and tiring.

road cut in the rock, which, in 1 hour's approx. of a rather toilsome ascent, brings you to the top of Umm El Biyara. Here we find the remains of an Edomite settlement, eight huge bell-shaped cisterns, and some Nabataean ruins, including a temple (or anyhow a sacred site) placed on the edge of the precipice. The climbing of this massif is to be exclusively undertaken together with a guide, with plenty of water and food, and only provided you are fit and wear the proper footgear.

99 Left above: in the wadi Thughra there is also this tower tomb, on two floors.

99 Right above: the terrace of the shrine on the 'Umm al Biyara, dug on the brink of the precipice.

99 Left below: the mysterious Monument of the Serpent, maybe a deity simulacrum.

99 Right below: fragment of a carved frieze, regarding the Nabataean sanctuary.

5 - MUGHAR AN-NASARA ***

This itinerary is recommended only to those who are both fascinated by ancient ruins and keen on long, difficult and uneasy walks. Moreover, the journey should be embarked upon in the coolest hours of the day.

From the tomb of Sextius Florentinus (p. 52), which ought to be taken as a reference behind you, you need to head north-east. In other words, you must go straight on, cross the river bed of Wadi Mataha a little upstream from the meeting point between this and the Wadi An Nasara, then turn right. You climb along one of the numerous paths initiated by goats, in the direction of a rocky outcrop perforated by ancient quarries and numerous graves. This, in fact, is Mughar An-Nasara, a sector of Petra outside the enceinte whose modern name (Caves of the Christians) comes from the many crosses dug on the monuments of the area. Bear in mind that the zone has never been either excavated or explored systematically, and that in the multi-coloured sandstone banks many treacherous ditch graves open. In the surroundings, you can observe numerous well preserved burials (a real catalogue of Nabataean architectonic types), sacred roads and courtyards dug out in the rock. The main attraction, however, is the **Suit of Armour Tomb,** whose façade, preceded by the usual rock-carved courtyard, is of the "double-cornice" type, while its attic is highlighted by four short pilasters with Nabataean capitals. In the spaces in between, two relief-sculptured Medusa heads stand out and, in the centre, a trophy of arms. Here you clearly see a suit of armour, the source of the name to the monument (dating from the second half of the I century b.C.): this decoration is the only one of its type attested at Petra. The visit to the surrounding area can even last a few hours; nevertheless, it is a good idea to keep an eye on your watch, because the walk back to the entrance gate of the archaeological area from here is quite long. Those who want to extend their exploration, from the Suit of Armour Tomb can go down towards the dry river bed of the Wadi Mataha, cross it and re-climb the opposite side until they reach the "House of Dorotheos" (see the following itinerary), and then return towards the Tomb of Sextius Florentinus (about 1 hour's walk).

100 Right: view of the Mughar an Nasara; Nasara means Nazarene, the name by which Arabs once called Christians.

100 Left: the Tomb of Armour, due to its coat of arms decoration and to the two Medusa Heads, it is absolutely unique in its genre.

101 Left: the Carmine Facade is an enigma for archeologists, but with its polychromatism veining it constitutes an authentic joy for lovers of photography. It may well be that the burial chamber was dug under the front courtyard and that it still has to be un-earthed.

6 - WADI MATAHA **/***

Even though not difficult, the proposed route should be undertaken in the coolest moments of the day, and with a good supply of water.
From the Tomb of Sextius Florentinus (p. 52) continue along the well-marked path which, proceeding into the valley of the Wadi Mataha, skirts the precipitous slopes of Gebel El Khubtha. About 10 or so m from the ground, along the mountain wall, you will clearly see a deep canalisation, obviously where one of Petra's main aqueducts ran. It is interesting to note how it picked up also the rainwater from each vertical crack in the mountain, permitting a thorough exploitation of the water resources. All the rocky versant is covered with a great number of hypogea, worship niches, cisterns, steps boldly carved for the maintenance of the aqueduct. However, there are only a few graves, certifying that this must have been a residential suburb of the city, even if it was situated outside the enceinte. The first structure of a certain interest you come across is the **Carmine Façade,** so-called after its spectacular polychromy. It is dug deep into the rock wall, and faced by what seems to be a vast court, delimited towards downhill by a partly destroyed wall, where a

flourishing grove of oleanders grows. The structure is of the pediment kind, with a nice Doric frieze of the Nabataean type, i.e. with the metopes substituted with slightly raised discs. What renders anomalous the monument is the fact that the door - as also an interior ambience – is missing. According to some, it is an uncompleted grave, but it is more likely (given the level of the finishing touches of the various architectural details) that its purpose was something else. In its surroundings, a big tank opens, whose sandy content was removed only recently, and today serves as a drinking trough for goats. Going on further, we finally meet with the fam **House of Dorotheos,** being a group of hypogea placed on several levels, and reachable by a steep ramp of steps. It must have been the home of a well-off family, enjoying all comforts, including some capacious, still perfectly functioning tanks (beware of their well-like entrances). Its name derives from, and is to be found in, two Greek inscriptions, discovered on the inner walls. The approx. ten-room complex includes even a private worship area, with a monolithic altar. The freshness that you breathe in the wider chamber - with the windows set out on

two floors - demonstrates how wise the habit of living in hypogeous ambiences was. Some rooms get light from windows carved in the rock, others have the door preceded by a sort of small terrace. It is not known whether originally the façades were enriched with architectural decorations or plastered.

From here we advise to return on one's steps, but the more athletic can go on even further, always along the slopes of the Gebel El Khubta, where other several rock houses show up. A modern stone bank bridles the irregular, no less than violent, floods of the Wadi Muthlim. The latter opens suddenly on the right: this is the inlet to the valley of the "Small Siq", where the waters of the Wadi Mousa flow, regimented by the Nabataeans

101 Right: two views of the so-called house of Dorotheos, one of the better conserved settlements in Petra. Of remarkable interest is the big room with doors and windows on two floors.

through the tunnel that opens close to the entrance of el Siq (p. 36). Entering the small gorge for a few metres (never during a rainstorm!), you discover one of Petra's best kept secrets, i.e. a very suggestive **rock shrine** dug into the walls of a giants' "pothole". You will notice various niches for worship (one is surmounted by a crescent, linked to the Al-Uzza cult) and betyles, but what is really surprising is the big aedicule sculpted on the side facing east. It consists in a small niche (where an image of a divinity was placed) embedded between two semi-columns joined together by a curvilinear pediment, in their turn placed between two tall pilaster strips crowned by capitals on which an architrave, adorned with two busts, leans. The effect is extraordinary, and invites one to silent contemplation. Climbing back up the deep valley until the tunnel, which is very exhausting (it requires repeated, short acts of clambering), is deeply advised against. From here it is worthwhile returning: head towards the Tomb of Sextius Florentinus and Petra's hollow. Good walkers (but it would be opportune to have a local guide), instead, can go back to Wadi Mousa for a further journey on foot of a couple of hours. From the exit of the Small Siq into the Wadi Mataha, you turn right and climb again the dry river bed of the torrent, then you pass the crevice of the Wadi Sidd El Ma'ajin, parallel to the Small Siq. You pass under the very dangerous arch of an aqueduct (probably from the Roman times) that used to take water to Petra from a big cistern (al Birka), and you ascend again the gorge of the Wadi Shab Qais, right-hand side tributary of the Wadi Mataha. You finally reach the built-up area of Wadi Mousa, close to the Petra Forum Hotel.

7- GEBEL EL KHUBTA **/***

This excursion and the following one are exclusively suggested both to those who will be wanting to say that at Petra they have seen "everything", and to the bravest walkers.
About a few dozens of metres before the grave of Sextius Florentinus (p. 52), the path coming from the Palace Tomb reaches a junction: the side-lane

102 Left: the most remarkable element in the rocky sanctuary of wadi Mataha is this big ritual aedicola , in whose central niche the simulacrum of the god was posed.

102, Centre: As a few lunar-crescent topped niches for devotionals seem to suggest, the shrine in the wadi Mataha must have been consecrated to the worship of Al Uzza, goddess of fertility.

102 Right: more

than for reaching the goal itself, the climb to the Gebel al Khubta is fascinating for the impression given by the procession road, for long bits cut out of the live rock.

103 Left: two foreshortenings of the wadi Muthlim, or Small Siq.

103 Right: it is very probable that the Niche of the Eagle is of the period of Roman domination.

turns right and immediately changes into an endless series of ramps of steps climbing to the top of Gebel El Khutba along a spectacular processional road. This led to one of the "high places of sacrifice" that seem to protect the old built-up area of Petra like a sort of mystical circle, but what really makes this straining climb interesting is the path itself – all cut in the rock – and the marvellous views to be enjoyed during the journey.
The route even passes under a sort of arc that in the past may have been barred with powerful wooden gates. The destination consists in a sacred area cut into the rock (far more modest, if

compared with that on Gebel Attuf), near which you will find also a spacious tank, still partially covered with a vault, and the ruins of some structures of difficult interpretation.

From here, different paths branch off (one brings you to a panoramic point where you can admire the Khasneh from above; another to the Urn Tomb), that you had better not try out unless you're with a local guide.

8 - THE SMALL SIQ ***

The Small Siq, or Wadi Muthlim, gathers the waters of the Wadi Mousa through the impressive cutting and tunnel dug by the Nabataeans on the right of the entrance to el Siq, to divert the disastrous, sudden floods of the torrent. Because of the extraordinary colours of the rocks, of the mysterious silence pervading the gorge, and the little size of some spectacular passages (where the walls opposite the canyon are about 1 m away!), this would be one of the most exciting routes in the area of Petra (described in detail in a tour guide published by the author of these texts in 1999). Unfortunately, recent floods have rendered it more impracticable than it used to be, and in some stretches even dangerous: we recommend, therefore, not to risk the descent of the Wadi.

Nevertheless, on the other side of the tunnel (absolutely do not cross it in case of rain or storms, because of the lightning and the deadly waves of the floods), on the left side of the cut you can see quite a steep, not very well laid out ramp, that allows you

to climb - with some exertion, though - to the rock plateau above, which, in the hottest hours of the day, changes into an authentic oven. Turning your back to the Wadi and looking in front of you, a little to the right, you will see at once a rock wall along which various niches and betyles were sculpted. The showiest one is the so-called **Niche of the Eagle**, a votive aedicule, which, with all likelihood, dates from Roman domination, since in the centre (between two thin pilaster strips, holding a sort of broken pediment) stands out a figure of a spread-eagle raptor, similar to those of the legion signs. From here we suggest you trace your steps.

AL BARID – THE "LITTLE PETRA"*

A few kilometres north of Wadi Mousa we find another archaeological area, much smaller compared with Petra, but quite interesting all the same: this is Al Barid, better known as "Little Petra". Though the destination can be reached also on foot (along the paved road, with a march of about 2 1/2 h; from Petra, ascending the Wadi Turkmanyyia, in at least 3 h), we warmly suggest to take a taxi, both going and coming back (the movement requires about 15 minutes and the expense is quite small). If you choose this solution, you can ask the driver to stop for a few minutes during the journey, to pay a short visit to the ruins of the crusaders' al Wu'eira castle, rising castled in a formidable position on the edge of a precipice. To wander through the ruins you must cross a modern gangway bridging the abyss, and substituting the original drawbridge. The fort, which the king of Jerusalem Badouin I decided to build around 1116, was known to crusaders as Li Vaux Moise and was part of the defensive system set up to control trade along the road linking Damascus with Cairo. Besieged several times with alternate success by Muslim armies, it fell at last in 1189, after Saladin had defeated the Christian armies in the Holy Land in the battle of Hattin. It is worthwhile remembering that this was the last Christian outpost to surrender.

The car will stop in a vast open space used as a parking area, where there is usually a tent and one can buy some souvenirs or, even better, quench one's thirst with some excellent local tea. Nearby there is an immense Nabataean cistern, the most capacious of those known in the area of Petra, but your attention shall at once focus on a small but elegant

104 Above: along the road that from Wadi Musa leads to al Barid one can notice this strange natural formation known as the 'Rock of the Elephant'.

104 Below: view of the fortress of Li Vaux Moise, strategically placed on the brink of a deep ravine.

façade of the pediment type, preceded by a short flight of steps; the door, embedded between two pilaster strips with Nabataean capitals, is surmounted by a pretty Doric Nabataean frieze and by a curvilinear pediment. Despite its aspect, it is believed not to be a tomb, since Al Barid was transit and trading area, or better a caravanserai where the big caravans heading for Petra could stop and let their dromedaries drink. Here merchants commuting between Arabia and the Mediterranean coasts stopped, and the goods dispatched to the markets of the nearby Nabataean capital were stocked. Under this respect, some authors have imagined that the pretty rocky structure might be a sort of guard-post, or "customs office" where the officials in charge of levying duties lived, but it is really difficult to say whether this hypothesis is grounded or not; according to others, providing a hastier hypothesis, it was a temple, in all cases dating from the first half of the I century A.D., as all the monuments at Little Petra. Shortly beyond, the surrounding rocky walls – that here form a sort of a natural amphitheatre – nearly touch each other, forming an extremely narrow fissure, about 10 m long, which in ancient times was defended by a portal. This sort of miniature Siq (it is actually called Siq Al Barid) ends up in a natural widening, dominated by another beautiful façade carved out of sandstone in an elevated position. Its aspect, with the two columns *in antis,* topped by the usual Nabataean capitals and by a sober frieze lacking all ornamentation, leads us to

105 Left: the elegant pediment facade of the temple situated at the entrance to the Siq al Barid.

105 Right: two foreshortenings of the Siq al Barid.

suppose that this was a **temple**, dedicated to the main Nabataean gods, Dushara and Al-Uzza. The hypothesis is realistic, also because in the interior no traces of loculi are to be found, and it seems logical that the caravans should be received in a secure location of the caravanserai by just a templar edifice.

Other cavities open out all around – tricliniar halls, above all, but also enormous cisterns – whilst a dizzy staircase ascends in a natural crevice to the left of the rocky temple. This and the other airy flights that we can notice a bit everywhere led to numerous canalisations - whose purpose was to convey rainwater - but also to the inevitable "high places of sacrifice", that here, as at Petra, were placed all around the settlement, constituting a sort of a protective, mystic ring.

If you are lucky enough to have all of Al Barid for yourselves, the silence of the place, the light shining from above amongst the crazily eroded stones, the nuances of the sandstone, cause the

106 Below Left: the facade of the temple with in antis columns.

106 Right: the vertiginous ramps of stairs dug into the Siq al Barid.

107 Two details of the frescoes conserved in the Painted House: one can detect three Cupids.

108-109 Another view of the temple in antis.

experience to be magic and really unforgettable: it is easy to imagine the ancient merchants animating these fresh and protected places, intent on contracting over a lot of spices, or on banqueting and discussing about the latest news. You can live anew such sensations shortly later, in the second natural widening of Siq al Barid, there where a stairway and a small gangway introduce you into the famous **Painted House**, which in reality is a tricliniar hall, whose walls still bear a part of their plaster, painted so as to imitate ashlar; on the arcosolium vault opening out in the back wall are precious and rare traces of a rich pictorial decoration, with racemes, flowers, vine shoots, birds of various species and cupids. One of these, identified with the young Pan, plays a piccolo, whilst a second one, perhaps Eros, is armed with his bow and arrows. Now, these ancient remains, blackened by smoke and damaged by the iconoclasts, may appear to be of very little importance; but one must imagine this, and many other analogous ambiences, when colours were brilliant, and the underlying caravanserai teemed with life. Moreover, the bunches of grapes make us imagine that vineyards must have been quite well known to Nabataeans, just as they probably appreciated wine (a historical fact also mentioned by the historian Strabo).

Any of you who are really in a hurry can now go back to where we started out from, whilst whoever has some extra time available can go on right to

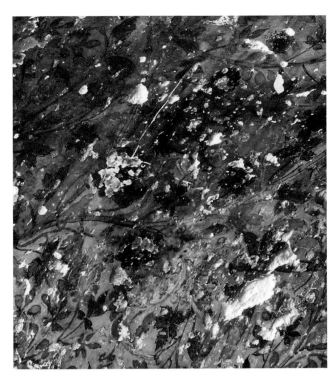

the very end of the gorge, where a dramatic stairway carved into a narrow fissure leads out of Al Barid (nearby there is also a "high place of sacrifice"); since the geography of the place is quite bumpy, in all cases it is not worthwhile going too far.

From Al Barid, following a path – a long one, but whose landscape is fascinating – you can reach el Deir (p. 71), but this exacting excursion should be undertaken only with a local guide. About 1 km south-east of Little Petra there are the remains of the Al Beidha (the White) prehistoric village, considered one of the most ancient human settlements of the whole Middle East; its visit is suggested only to those who are keen on archaeology and to scholars.

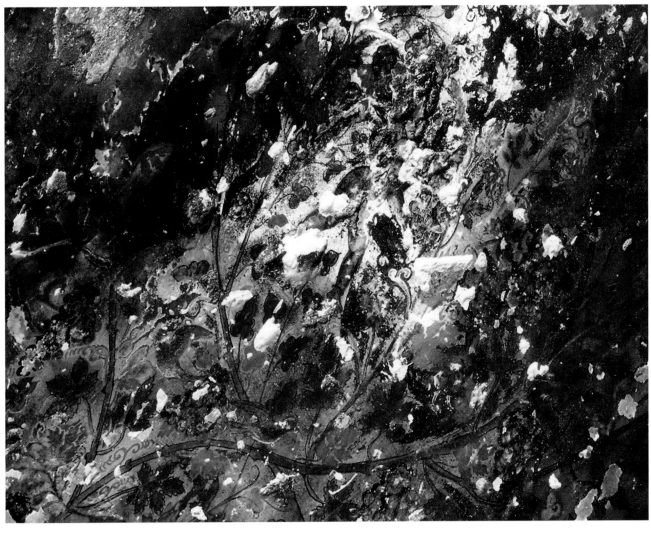

GLOSSARY

Acroterium: in classical architecture, a decorative element, vase, sphere or other item, placed at the highest point and at the sides of the pediment. It can also have a more complex form -for example, be a statue-.

Aniconic: that does not allow the use of images, in particular those taken from the surrounding world.

Arcosolium: niche with an arched ceiling, usually seen inside funerary temples or tombs, within which a sarcophagus was placed.

Attic: the part of a construction over and above the ceiling of the building – or the entablature in a temple – having an ornamental function.

Betyle: non-figurative image of the Nabataean gods. It is usually in the form of a simple solid body, like a cube, a parallelepiped, a cylinder, an egg or a sphere. This word literally means 'house of the god'.

Biclinium: banquet hall similar to the triclinium, but in which only two tricliniar beds are to be found, usually placed opposite each other on the two long sides of the chamber.

Entablature (or trabeation): architectural element standing on columns composed of the architrave, frieze and the cornice.

Exedra: an architectonic structure with a semi-circular circumference.

Frieze: decorative element of elongated form, painted or sculpted. Usually it is a part of the entablature.

Hellenism: historical period comprised between the death of Alexander the Great -323 b. C. - and the Roman conquest of Egypt -31 b. C.-. During those three centuries *Greek art was influenced by the oriental one and acquired* a marked tendency to realism, till it exceeded in patheticalness.

Intercolumniation: the space comprised between two columns.

In antis: a term indicating to a temple which has two or more columns in its façade, comprised between two pillars situated at the end of the lateral walls of the building.

Metopes: in the entablature of the Doric order, each of the spaces comprised between one triglyph and another with usually adorned with statues in relief or with simple disks.

Nymphaeum: originally, sanctuary of the Nymphs, later semi-circular construction or of elliptic form, usually apsidal, with niches and a big central fountain, not rarely embellished with statues.

Patera: a cup in the form of a large and low bowl, used in ancient times during sacred libations. Stylised, it became a decorative element in architecture, where it often substitutes the metope.

Pediment: an architectonic element of triangular form, with two slopes situated on the crown of buildings, doors, windows and niches.

Pilaster: synonym of pilaster-strip.

Pilaster-strip: a decorative architectonic element, constituted by half a column or half a pilaster, protruding from the line of the wall and surmounted by a half capital.

Pronaos: the covered spaces between the columns of the façade and the inside of a temple or building.

Raceme: a decorative element in the form of a plant branch.

Sub-structure: a wall structure constituting the supporting base of a building above it.

Temenos: out door area, delimited by a sacred precinct, where religious ceremonies took place.

Tetrastyle: any temple with four columns in its façade.

Tholos: a circular temple with conic covering.

Tympanum: a triangular, vertical architectonic element, comprised between the slopes of the pediment and the line of the architrave. It can be plain or decorated with reliefs or sculptural groups of statues.

Transenna: a architectonic element present in the most ancient Christian churches, in the form of a wooden or stone parapet that divided the presbytery and the apses from the nave.

Triclinium: banquet hall, with three benches or tricliniar beds aligned as the letter P, along the walls, on which guests would stretch themselves out on a side.

Triglyph: in the Doric order entablature, the decorative element constituted by a tablet furrowed by two vertical flutes or grooves, alternating with the metopes.

Vestibule: the portico that precedes the cell in a temple.

BASIC BIBLIOGRAPHY

Augé C. and Dentzer J-M., Petra. The Rose-red City, Trieste 1999.

Bienkowski P. -editions -, The Art of Jordan: Treasures from an Ancient Land, Liverpool 1991.

Bourbon F., Petra. Guida archeologica alla città scolpita nella roccia, Vercelli 1999.

Browning I., Petra, London 1982.

Gagos T. -editions- , The Carbonized Papyri from Petra, University of Michigan 1994.

Guzzo M.G.A. and Schneider E.E., Petra, Milan1997.

Harding Lankester G., The Antiquities of Jordan, Londra 1959.

Howard T., Treks and Climbs in the Mountains of Wadi Rum and Petra, Amman 1987.

Joukowsky M. S., Petra Great Temple, Providence RI 1998.

Keiser H., Petra dei Nabatei, Tourin 1972.

Lyttlelton M., Baroque Architecture in Classical Antiquity, London 1974.

Markoe G.-editions- , Petra Rediscovered, London 2003.

Maqsood R., Petra: a Travellers' Guide, Lebanon 1996.

McKenzie J., The Architecture of Petra, Oxford 1990.

Rostovtzeff, Città carovaniere, Bari 1971.

Taylor J, Petra, Amman 2005.

Zayadine F.-editions- , Petra and the Caravan Cities, Amman 1990.

PHOTOGRAPHIC CREDITS: